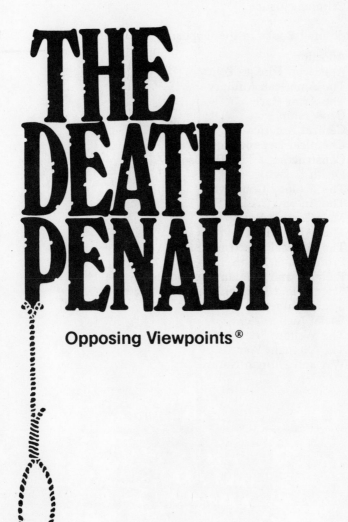

THE DEATH PENALTY

Opposing Viewpoints®

Other Books of Related Interest in the Opposing Viewpoints Series:

America's Prisons
Crime & Criminals
Criminal Justice

Additional Books in the Opposing Viewpoints Series:

Abortion
American Foreign Policy
The American Military
The Arms Race
Censorship
Central America
Chemical Dependency
Constructing a Life Philosophy
Death & Dying
The Ecology Controversy
The Energy Crisis
Male/Female Roles
The Middle East
The Political Spectrum
Problems of Death
Religion and Human Experience
Science and Religion
Sexual Values
Social Justice
The Welfare State
The Vietnam War
War and Human Nature

THE DEATH PENALTY

Opposing Viewpoints®

David L. Bender & Bruno Leone, *Series Editors*

Bonnie Szumski, Lynn Hall,
& Susan Bursell, *Book Editors*

OPPOSING VIEWPOINTS SERIES ®

Greenhaven Press
577 Shoreview Park Road
St. Paul, Minnesota 55126

Library of Congress Cataloging-in-Publication Data

The Death Penalty
  (Opposing viewpoints series)
  Includes bibliographies and index.
  Summary: Presents opposing viewpoints on the purpose, morality, deterrent influence, and application of the death penalty.
    1. Capital punishment—United States—Addresses, essays, lectures. [1. Capital punishment—Addresses, essays, lectures] I. Szumski, Bonnie, 1958-
II. Hall, Lynn, 1949-   . III. Bursell, Susan,
1951-   . IV. Series.
HV8699.U5D4   1986   364.6'6'0973   86-303
ISBN 0-089908-381-1 (lib. bdg.)
ISBN 0-089908-356-0 (pbk.)

"Congress shall make no law...
abridging the freedom of speech,
or of the press."

First Amendment to the US Constitution

The basic foundation of our democracy is the first amendment
guarantee of freedom of expression. The *Opposing Viewpoints
Series* is dedicated to the concept of this basic freedom and the
idea that it is more important to practice it than to enshrine it.

Contents

Why Consider Opposing Viewpoints?

"It is better to debate a question without settling it than to settle a question without debating it."

Joseph Joubert (1754-1824)

The Importance of Examining Opposing Viewpoints

The purpose of the Opposing Viewpoints books, and this book in particular, is to present balanced, and often difficult to find, opposing points of view on complex and sensitive issues.

Probably the best way to become informed is to analyze the positions of those who are regarded as experts and well studied on issues. It is important to consider every variety of opinion in an attempt to determine the truth. Opinions from the mainstream of society should be examined. But also important are opinions that are considered radical, reactionary, or minority as well as those stigmatized by some other uncomplimentary label. An important lesson of history is the eventual acceptance of many unpopular and even despised opinions. The ideas of Socrates, Jesus, and Galileo are good examples of this.

Readers will approach this book with their own opinions on the issues debated within it. However, to have a good grasp of one's own viewpoint, it is necessary to understand the arguments of those with whom one disagrees. It can be said that those who do not completely understand their adversary's point of view do not fully understand their own.

A persuasive case for considering opposing viewpoints has been presented by John Stuart Mill in his work *On Liberty*. When examining controversial issues it may be helpful to reflect on this suggestion:

> The only way in which a human being can make some approach to knowing the whole of a subject, is by hearing what can be said about it by persons of every variety of opinion, and studying all modes in which it can be looked at by every character of mind. No wise man ever acquired his wisdom in any mode but this.

Analyzing Sources of Information

The Opposing Viewpoints Series includes diverse materials taken from magazines, journals, books, and newspapers, as well as statements and position papers from a wide range of individuals, organizations and governments. This broad spectrum of sources helps to develop patterns of thinking which are open to the consideration of a variety of opinions.

Pitfalls to Avoid

A pitfall to avoid in considering opposing points of view is that of regarding one's own opinion as being common sense and the most rational stance and the point of view of others as being only opinion and naturally wrong. It may be that another's opinion is correct and one's own is in error.

Another pitfall to avoid is that of closing one's mind to the opinions of those with whom one disagrees. The best way to approach a dialogue is to make one's primary purpose that of understanding the mind and arguments of the other person and not that of enlightening him or her with one's own solutions. More can be learned by listening than speaking.

It is my hope that after reading this book the reader will have a deeper understanding of the issues debated and will appreciate the complexity of even seemingly simple issues on which good and honest people disagree. This awareness is particularly important in a democratic society such as ours where people enter into public debate to determine the common good. Those with whom one disagrees should not necessarily be regarded as enemies, but perhaps simply as people who suggest different paths to a common goal.

Developing Basic Reading and Thinking Skills

In this book, carefully edited opposing viewpoints are purposely placed back to back to create a running debate; each viewpoint is preceded by a short quotation that best expresses the author's main argument. This format instantly plunges the reader into the midst of a controversial issue and greatly aids that reader in mastering the basic skill of recognizing an author's point of view.

A number of basic skills for critical thinking are practiced in the activities that appear throughout the books in the series. Some of the skills are:

Evaluating Sources of Information   The ability to choose from among alternative sources the most reliable and accurate source in relation to a given subject.

Separating Fact from Opinion   The ability to make the basic distinction between factual statements (those that can be demonstrated or verified empirically) and statements of opinion (those that are beliefs or attitudes that cannot be proved).

Identifying Stereotypes   The ability to identify oversimplified, exaggerated descriptions (favorable or unfavorable) about people and insulting statements about racial, religious or national groups, based upon misinformation or lack of information.

Recognizing Ethnocentrism   The ability to recognize attitudes or opinions that express the view that one's own race, culture, or group is inherently superior, or those attitudes that judge another culture or group in terms of one's own.

It is important to consider opposing viewpoints and equally important to be able to critically analyze those viewpoints. The activities in this book are designed to help the reader master these thinking skills. Statements are taken from the book's viewpoints and the reader is asked to analyze them. This technique aids the reader in developing skills that not only can be applied to the viewpoints in this book, but also to situations where opinionated spokespersons comment on controversial issues. Although the activities are helpful to the solitary reader, they are most useful when the reader can benefit from the interaction of group discussion.

Using this book and others in the series should help readers develop basic reading and thinking skills. These skills should improve the reader's ability to understand what they read. Readers should be better able to separate fact from opinion, substance from rhetoric and become better consumers of information in our media-centered culture.

This volume of the Opposing Viewpoints Series does not advocate a particular point of view. Quite the contrary! The very nature of the book leaves it to the reader to formulate the opinions he or she finds most suitable. My purpose as publisher is to see that this is made possible by offering a wide range of viewpoints which are fairly presented.

David L. Bender
Publisher

Introduction

"It is but law that when the red drops have been spilled upon the ground they cry aloud for fresh blood."

Aeschylus, *Libation Bearers* (458 BC)

"Our ancestors . . . . purged their guilt by banishment, not death. And by so doing, they stopped that endless vicious cycle of murder and revenge."

Euripides, *Orestes* (408 BC)

Legal execution—society's ultimate sanction—has existed as long as has human culture. One of the first written codes of law, composed by Hammurabi of Babylonia and carved on a stone column nearly four thousand years ago, includes death as an appropriate punishment. In most cultures, this sentence is reserved for the most severe crimes—murder, violent sexual assault, and treason. But in some times and places, in both simple and sophisticated societies, punishments for many crimes have been startlingly severe, even including death for stealing a loaf of bread or writing derogatory songs about notables.

Today more than one-half of the world's nations use capital punishment—some commonly, some infrequently. Iran, for example, has been the site of more than 5000 legal executions since 1979. China recently held public mass executions by firing squad in an effort to reduce violent crime. Japan prescribes the death penalty for thirteen different crimes. In Ireland, capital punishment is legal, but the last state-sanctioned execution was in 1954. In the United States capital punishment is legal in most states, but its actual imposition occurs only rarely and only after lengthy, automatic, processes of legal appeals.

Even in some countries which have abolished the death penalty for most offenses, there are crimes for which they continue to use this ultimate punishment. In Morocco, attempted assassination of the King, murder, and arson are capital crimes. In Argentina, political rebellion is grounds for execution. Israel has retained it for treason and war crimes. The legislative bodies of these countries believe that some crimes call for death as just punishment or retribution for the crime committed or as a deterrent to future crimes of a similar nature.

13

A few countries, notably Sweden, Denmark, Finland, and Portugal, have not allowed capital punishment for decades. In 1957, the United Nations began moving toward a policy urging the world-wide abolition of capital punishment on the grounds that "every human has an inherent right to life." Numerous individual countries have been also moving in this direction. Canada abolished the death penalty in 1976. Since 1981, it is no longer possible in France for criminals to be executed, a fact deplored by many of those who believe that death is a just and effective punishment but applauded by those who regard such executions as barbaric and immoral. Despite a dramatic rise in terrorism and violent crime, Britain's Parliament voted decisively in 1983 not to reinstate the death penalty which they had abolished in 1965.

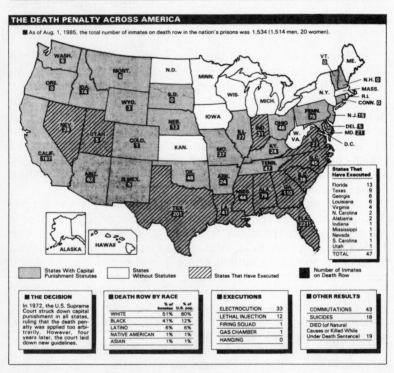

THE DEATH PENALTY ACROSS AMERICA

As of Aug. 1, 1985, the total number of inmates on death row in the nation's prisons was 1,534 (1,514 men, 20 women).

States That Have Executed

Florida	13
Texas	9
Georgia	6
Louisiana	6
Virginia	4
N. Carolina	2
Alabama	2
Indiana	1
Mississippi	1
Nevada	1
S. Carolina	1
Utah	1
TOTAL	47

States With Capital Punishment Statutes · States Without Statutes · States That Have Executed · Number of Inmates on Death Row

THE DECISION

In 1972, the U.S. Supreme Court struck down capital punishment in all states, ruling that the death penalty was applied too arbitrarily. However, four years later, the court laid down new guidelines.

DEATH ROW BY RACE

	% of Inmates	% of U.S. pop.
WHITE	51%	80%
BLACK	41%	12%
LATINO	6%	6%
NATIVE AMERICAN	1%	1%
ASIAN	1%	1%

EXECUTIONS

ELECTROCUTION	33
LETHAL INJECTION	12
FIRING SQUAD	1
GAS CHAMBER	1
HANGING	0

OTHER RESULTS

COMMUTATIONS	43
SUICIDES	18
DIED (of Natural Causes or Killed While Under Death Sentence)	19

While some cheer the move to abolish capital punishment, others are convinced that it is a necessary weapon for society to wield in defense of itself. The relatively recent phenomenon of vicious mass murders and the alarming increase in world terrorism are two of the extreme trends to which supporters of the death penalty point. These crimes seem to many to require the certainty of the most severe form of retaliation in order to increase the risk for the murderers and possibly reduce it for the rest of society.

The viewpoints in this book revolve around two of the most central issues in the capital punishment debate—Is the death penalty moral? and Does the death penalty deter crime? In addition, the editors have included six views of the death penalty from the past three centuries, viewpoints old in time and literary style but as contemporary as today in the concerns expressed. Finally, a chapter inspired by today's headlines debates whether the death penalty should be used in cases of treason. The United States has been the setting for several sensational treason trials in the twentieth century, all of which stirred debate about capital punishment. This final chapter brings together opposing views on three of them, those of Sacco and Vanzetti in the 1920s, Julius and Ethel Rosenberg in the 1950s, and John Walker in the 1980s.

The Death Penalty: Opposing Viewpoints includes ideas drawn from the works of philosophers, criminologists, religious leaders, government officials, journalists, and even convicted criminals. As with all volumes in the Opposing Viewpoints Series, the opinions of these authors are presented without editorial comment or interference. The reader, therefore, is left to analyze and evaluate the arguments about this timely issue and to draw his or her own conclusions.

Three Centuries of Debate on the Death Penalty

"I must beg leave to say, that those who shew no mercy should find none; and if Hanging will not restrain them, Hanging them in Chains, and Starving them . . . or breaking them on the wheel . . . should."

The Death Penalty Will Discourage Crime, 1701

Paper Presented Before the House of Parliament

In eighteenth-century England, some 200 crimes were punishable by death including pickpocketing and petty theft. Many people were attempting to reform this excess of executions by reducing the sentences for many offenses. Others believed, however, that the death penalty should continue to be rigorously applied for heinous crimes. In the following viewpoint, the author states that punishments should remain severe and perhaps be even more so. He argues that keeping the death penalty a very real threat is the only way to stop people from committing violent and offensive crimes.

As you read, consider the following:

1. Why does the author believe the death penalty must be used "steadily and impartially"?
2. On what does the author base his argument that there should be differences in the degrees of punishments?
3. What does the author say society should be careful of when applying the death penalty?

Hanging Not Punishment Enough for Murtherers, Highway Men, and House-Breakers. London: A. Balwin, 1701.

I am sensible, That the *English* Clemency and Mildness appear eminently in our Laws and Constitutions; but since it is found that *Ill* Men are grown so much more incorrigible, than in our fore-fathers Days, is it not fit that *Good* Men should grow less merciful to them, since gentler Methods are ineffectual?

I acknowledge also, That the Spirit of Christianity disposes us to Patience and Forbearance, insomuch that when the *Roman* Emperors began to grow Christian, we are informed, That most Capital Punishments were taken away, and turned into others less Sanguinary; either that they might have longer time for Repentance, (an Indulgence agreeable to the Zeal and Piety of those Good Ages) or that the length and continuance of their Punishment might be more Exemplary. And I acknowledge with the Wise *Quintilian, That if Ill men could be made Good, as, it must be granted, they sometimes may, it is for the Interest of the Commonwealth, that they should rather be spared than punished.* And I know, that 'tis frequently alledg'd, That you take away a Better thing, and that is a Man's Life, for that which is worse, and that is, your Money and Goods; but tho' this be speciously enough urged, yet I doubt not, but the Publick Safety and Happiness may lawfully and reasonably be secured by this way, if it can by no other. . . .

Show No Mercy to the Merciless

I must beg leave to say, that those who shew no mercy should find none; and if Hanging will not restrain them, Hanging them in Chains, and Starving them, or (if Murtherers and Robbers at the same time, or Night incendiaries) breaking them on the Wheel, or Whipping them to Death, a *Roman* Punishment should.

I know that Torments so unusual and unknown to us may at first surprize us, and appear unreasonable; but I hope easily to get over that difficulty, and make it appear upon Examination, that *that* will be the more probable way to secure us from our fears of them, and the means of preserving great numbers of them, who now yearly by an easie Death are taken off at the Gallows. For to Men so far corrupted in their Principles and Practices, and that have no expectations beyond the Grave (for such, I fear, is the case of most of them) no Argument will be so cogent, as Pain in an intense degree; and a few such Examples made, will be so terrifying, that I persuade myself it would be a Law but seldom put in Execution.

The Death Penalty Must Be Used

But then I must add, that I fear it will not have its due effects, if it be too often dispens'd with; since *that* will be apt to give ground to every Offender, to hope he may be of the number of *those*, who shall escape, and so the good end of the Law will be defeated. For if Favour or Affection, or a Man's being of a good Family, or Money can prevail, and take off the Penalty of the

Statute; if it be not executed steadily and impartially, with an exact hand (still giving allowance for extraordinary Cases) it will serve to little purpose, since many will be found (as ill men easily flatter themselves) who will not fear a Law, that has sharp Teeth indeed, but does but sometimes bite. And this, I believe, must be allowed to be the only way to root out our Native Enemies, as they truly are; as might lately have been seen in a Neighbouring Kingdom, where severity, without the least mixture of mercy, did so sweep High-way Men out of the Nation, that it has been confidently said, that a Man might some time since have *openly* carried his Money without fear of losing it. That he cannot *now*, is to be charged upon their great numbers of Soldiers, without Employment and Plunder, and in poor pitiful Pay; and, it may be, on the very great necessities of the People, and make 'em desperate and careless of their Lives.

'Tis a Rule in Civil Law, and Reason, *That the Punishment should not exceed the fault.* If Death then be due to a Man, who surreptitiously steals the Value of Five Shillings (as it is made by a late Statute) surely *He* who puts me in fear of my Life, and breaks the King's Peace, and it may be, murthers me at last, and burns my House, deserves another sort of Censure; and if the one must die, the other should be made to *feel himself die....*

Severe Penalties Prevent Crime

In England, Germany, and France, a man knows, that if he commit murder, every person around him will, from that instant, become his enemy, and use every means to seize him and bring him to justice. He knows that he will be immediately carried to prison, and put to an ignominious death, amidst the execrations of his countrymen. Impressed with these sentiments, and with the natural horror for murder which such sentiments augment, the polulace of those countries hardly ever have recourse to stabbing in their accidental quarrels, however they may be inflamed with anger and rage. The lowest black-guard in the streets of London will not draw a knife against an antagonist far superior to himself in strength. He will fight him fairly with his fists as long as he can, and bear the severest drubbing, rather than use a means of defence which is held in detestation by his countrymen, and which would bring him to the gallows.

Dr. Moore, *The Opinions of Different Authors Upon the Punishment of Death,* 1812.

The frequent Repetitions of the same Crimes, even in defiance of the present Laws in being, is a just ground of enacting somewhat more terrible; and indeed seems to challenge and require it.

Farther still; at the *last great day* doubtless there will be degrees of Torment, proportionable to Mens guilt and sin here; and I can see no reason why we may not imitate the Divine justice, and inflict an Animadversion suitable to such enormous Offenders.

And this, I am persuaded, will best answer the End of Sanguinary Laws, which are not *chiefly* intended to punish the present Criminal, but to hinder others from being so; and on that account Punishments in the Learned Languages are called *Examples*, as being design'd to be such to all mankind. . . .

Careful of Shedding Human Blood

Still I am sensible, that tho' I argue for severity, in general we ought to be tender of shedding human blood; For *there is such a Consanguinity and Relation between all mankind, that no one ought to hurt another, unless for some good end to be obtain'd.* And *Bodily Punishment,* as the Civilian well observes, *is greater than any Pecuniary mulcts;* and every Man knows that he who loses his Life, is a much greater sufferer than he whose Goods are confiscated, or is Fined in the most unreasonable manner in the World.

But my design is not, that Man's blood *should* be shed, but that it should *not;* and I verily believe, that for *Five* Men Condemned and Executed *now,* you would hardly have *one then.* For those Men out of Terror of such a Law, would ('tis to be hoped) either apply themselves to honest Labour and Industry; or else would remove to our *Plantations,* where they are wanted, and so many useful Hands would not be yearly lost.

But I must add, That *it is not fit, that men in Criminal Causes,* as the Civil Law well directs, *should be condemned, unless the Evidence be clearer than the mid-day Sun;* and no Man should expire in such horrid Agonies, for whose Innocence there is the least pretense.

"The punishment of death has never prevented determined men from injuring society."

The Death Penalty Will Not Discourage Crime, 1764

Cesare Beccaria

An Italian criminologist, Cesare Beccaria lived and died in the 1700s. He influenced local economic reforms and stimulated penal reform throughout Europe. In 1764 he published *Essay on Crimes and Punishments*, one of the first arguments against capital punishment and inhumane treatment of criminals. In the following viewpoint, Mr. Beccaria condemns capital punishment on several grounds, including that it is not a deterrent to crime and is irrevocable.

As you read, consider the following questions:

1. Why does the author believe that the death penalty may be justified if a man is a threat to government?
2. What does an execution inspire in others, according to the author? What does he say about this reaction?
3. What does the author say about life imprisonment?

Cesare Beccaria, *An Essay On Crimes and Punishments*, originally published in London by F. Newberry, 1775.

The useless profusion of punishments, which has never made men better, induces me to enquire, whether the punishment of *death* be really just or useful in a well governed state? What *right*, I ask, have men to cut the throats of their fellow-creatures? Certainly not that on which the sovereignty and laws are founded. The laws, as I have said before, are only the sum of the smallest portions of the private liberty of each individual, and represent the general will, which is the aggregate of that of each individual. Did any one ever give to others the right of taking away his life? Is it possible, that in the smallest portions of the liberty of each, sacrificed to the good of the public, can be contained the greatest of all good, life? If it were so, how shall it be reconciled to the maxim which tells us, that a man has no right to kill himself? Which he certainly must have, if he could give it away to another.

But the punishment of death is not authorized by any right; for I have demonstrated that no such right exists. It is therefore a war of a whole nation against a citizen, whose destruction they consider as necessary, or useful to the general good. But if I can further demonstrate, that it is neither necessary nor useful, I shall have gained the cause of humanity.

Only One Reason for the Death Penalty

The death of a citizen cannot be necessary, but in one case. When, though deprived of his liberty, he has such power and connections as may endanger the security of the nation; when his existence may produce a dangerous revolution in the established form of government. But even in this case, it can only be necessary when a nation is on the verge of recovering or losing its liberty; or in times of absolute anarchy, when the disorders themselves hold the place of laws. But in a reign of tranquillity; in a form of government approved by the united wishes of the nation; in a state well fortified from enemies without, and supported by strength within, and opinion, perhaps more efficacious; where all power is lodged in the hands of a true sovereign; where riches can purchase pleasures and not authority, there can be no necessity for taking away the life of a subject.

If the experience of all ages be not sufficient to prove, that the punishment of death has never prevented determined men from injuring society; if the example of the Romans; if twenty years reign of Elizabeth, empress of Russia, in which she gave the fathers of their country an example more illustrious than many conquests bought with blood; if, I say, all this be not sufficient to persuade mankind, who always suspect the voice of reason, and who choose rather to be led by authority, let us consult human nature in proof of my assertion.

It is not the intenseness of the pain that has the greatest effect on the mind, but its continuance; for our sensibility is more easily and more powerfully affected by weak but repeated impressions, than by a violent, but momentary, impulse. The power of habits is universal over every sensible being. As it is by that we learn to speak, to walk, and to satisfy our necessities, so the ideas of morality are stamped on our minds by repeated impressions. The death of a criminal is a terrible but momentary spectacle, and therefore a less efficacious method of deterring others, than the continued example of a man deprived of his liberty, condemned, as a beast of burthen, to repair, by his labour, the injury he has done to society. *If I commit such a crime,* says the spectator to himself, *I shall be reduced to that miserable condition for the rest of my life.* A much more powerful preventive than the fear of death, which men always behold in distant obscurity.

The Effect of Violence Is Momentary

The terrors of death make so slight an impression, that it has not force enough to withstand the forgetfulness natural to mankind, even in the most essential things; especially when assisted by the passions. Violent impressions surprise us, but their effect is momentary; they are fit to produce those revolutions which instantly transform a common man into a Lacedaemonian or a Persian; but in a free and quiet government they ought to be rather frequent than strong.

A Dead Man Is Good for Nothing

It hath long since been observed, that a man after he is hanged is good for nothing, and that punishment invented for the good of society, ought to be useful to society. It is evident, that a score of stout robbers, condemned for life to some public work, would serve the state in their punishment, and that hanging them is a benefit to nobody but the executioner. . . .

The Romans never condemned a citizen to death, unless for crimes which concerned the safety of the state. These our masters, our first legislators, were careful of the blood of their fellow citizens; but we are extravagant with the blood of ours. . . .

The sword of justice is in our hands, but we ought rather to blunt than to sharpen its edge. It remains within its sheath in the presence of kings, to inform us that it ought seldom to be drawn.

Commentary on Cesare Beccaria, attributed to Voltaire, c. 1770.

The execution of a criminal is, to the multitude, a spectacle, which in some excites compassion mixed with indignation. These sentiments occupy the mind much more than that salutary terror which the laws endeavour to inspire; but in the contemplation of continued suffering, terror is the only, or a least predominant sensation. The severity of a punishment should be just sufficient to excite compassion in the spectators, as it is intended more for them than for the criminal.

A punishment, to be just, should have only that degree of severity which is sufficient to deter others. Now there is no man, who upon the least reflection, would put in competition and total and perpetual loss of his liberty, with the greatest advantages he could possibly obtain in consequence of a crime. Perpetual slavery, then, has in it all that is necessary to deter the most hardened and determined, as much as the punishment of death. I say it has more. There are many who can look upon death with intrepidity and firmness; some through fanaticism, and others through vanity, which attends us even to the grave; others from a desperate resolution, either to get rid of their misery, or cease to live: but fanaticism and vanity forsake the criminal in slavery, in chains and fetters, in an iron cage; and despair seems rather the beginning than the end of their misery. The mind, by collecting itself and uniting all its force, can, for a moment, repel assailing grief; but its most vigorous efforts are insufficient to resist perpetual wretchedness.

In all nations, where death is used as a punishment, every example supposes a new crime committed. Whereas in perpetual slavery, every criminal affords a frequent and lasting example; and if it be necessary that men should often be witnesses of the power of the laws, criminals should often be put to death; but this supposes a frequency of crimes; and from hence this punishment will cease to have its effect, so that it must be useful and useless at the same time.

Slavery and the Death Penalty

I shall be told, that perpetual slavery is as painful a punishment as death, and therefore as cruel. I answer, that if all the miserable moments in the life of a slave were collected into one point, it would be a more cruel punishment than any other; but these are scattered through his whole life, whilst the pain of death exerts all its force in a moment. There is also another advantage in the punishment of slavery, which is, that it is more terrible to the spectator than to the sufferer himself; for the spectator considers the sum of all his wretched moments, whilst the sufferer, by the misery of the present, is prevented from thinking of the future. All evils are increased by the imagination, and the sufferer finds resources and consolations, of which the spectators are ignorant; who judge by their own sensibility of what passes in a mind, by habit grown callous to misfortune.

Let us, for a moment, attend to the reasoning of a robber or assassin, who is deterred from violating the laws by the gibbet or the wheel. I am sensible, that to develop the sentiments of one's own heart, is an art which education only can teach: but although a villain may not be able to give a clear account of his principles,

25

they nevertheless influence his conduct. He reasons thus:

> What are these laws, that I am bound to respect, which make so great a difference between me and the rich man? He refuses me the farthing I ask of him, and excuses himself, by bidding me have recourse to labour with which he is unacquainted. Who made these laws? The rich and the great, who never deigned to visit the miserable hut of the poor; who have never seen him dividing a piece of mouldly bread, amidst the cries of his famished children and the tears of his wife. Let us break those ties, fatal to the greatest part of mankind, and only useful to a few indolent tyrants. Let us attack injustice at its source. I will return to my natural state of independence. I shall live free and happy on the fruits of my courage and industry. A day of pain and repentance may come, but it will be short; and for an hour of grief I shall enjoy years of pleasure and liberty. King of a small number, as determined as myself, I will correct the mistakes of fortune; and I shall see those tyrants grow pale and tremble at the sight of him, whom, with insulting pride, they would not suffer to rank with their dogs and horses.

Religion then presents itself to the mind of this lawless villain, and promising him almost a certainty of eternal happiness upon the easy terms of repentance, contributes much to lessen the horror of the last scene of the tragedy.

Horrible Punishments Serve No Purpose

A government that persists in retaining these horrible punishments can only assign one reason in justification of their conduct: that they have already so degraded and brutalized the habits of the people, that they cannot be restrained by any moderate punishments.

Are more atrocities committed in those countries where such punishments are unknown? Certainly not: the most savage banditti are always to be found under laws the most severe, and it is no more than what might be expected. The fate with which they are threatened hardens them to the sufferings of others as well as to their own. They know that they can expect no lenity, and they consider their acts of cruelty as retaliations.

Jeremy Bentham, *The Opinions of Different Authors On the Punishment of Death*, 1809.

But he who foresees, that he must pass a great number of years, even his whole life, in pain and slavery; a slave to those laws by which he was protected; in sight of his fellow citizens, with whom he lives in freedom and society; makes an useful comparison between those evils, the uncertainty of his success, and the shortness of the time in which he shall enjoy the fruits of his transgression. The example of those wretches continually before his eyes, make a much greater impression on him than a punishment, which, instead of correcting, makes him more obdurate.

The punishment of death is pernicious to society, from the example of barbarity it affords. If the passions, or the necessity of war, have taught men to shed the blood of their fellow creatures, the laws, which are intended to moderate the ferocity of mankind, should not increase it by examples of barbarity, the more horrible, as this punishment is usually attended with formal pageantry. Is it not absurd, that the laws, which detest and punish homicide, should, in order to prevent murder, publicly commit murder themselves? What are the true and most useful laws? Those compacts and conditions which all would propose and observe, in those moments when private interest is silent, or combined with that of the public. What are the natural sentiments of every person concerning the punishment of death? We may read them in the contempt and indignation with which every one looks on the executioner, who is nevertheless an innocent executor of the public will; a good citizen, who contributes to the advantage of society; the instrument of the general security within, as good as soldiers are without. What then is the origin of this contradiction? Why is this sentiment of mankind indelible, to the scandal of reason? It is, that in a secret corner of the mind, in which the original impressions of nature are still preserved, men discover a sentiment which tells them, that their lives are not lawfully in the power of any one, but of that necessity only, which with its iron scepter rules the universe.

Dragging Criminals to Death

What must men think, when they see wise magistrates and grave ministers of justice, with indifference and tranquillity, dragging a criminal to death, and whilst a wretch trembles with agony, expecting the fatal stroke, the judge, who has condemned him, with the coldest insensibility, and perhaps with no small gratification from the exertion of his authority, quits his tribunal to enjoy the comforts and pleasures of life? They will say,

> Ah! those cruel formalities of justice are a cloak to tyranny, they are a secret language, a solemn veil, intended to conceal the sword by which we are sacrificed to the insatiable idol of despotism. Murder, which they would represent to us as an horrible crime, we see practiced by them without repugnance, or remorse. Let us follow their example. A violent death appeared terrible in their descriptions, but we see that it is the affair of a moment. It will be still less terrible to him, who not expecting it, escapes almost all the pain.

Such is the fatal, though absurd reasoning of men who are disposed to commit crimes; on whom, the abuse of religion has more influence than religion itself.

If it be objected, that almost all the nations in all ages have punished certain crimes with death, I answer, that the force of these examples vanishes, when opposed to truth, against which prescription is urged in vain. The history of mankind is an immense sea of errors, in which a few obscure truths may here and there be found.

But human sacrifices have also been common in almost all nations. That some societies only, either few in number, or for a very short time, abstained from the punishment of death, is rather favourable to my argument, for such is the fate of great truths, that their duration is only as a flash of lightning in the long and dark night of error. The happy time is not yet arrived, when truth, as falsehood has been hitherto, shall be the portion of the greatest number.

"We show . . . our regard for [human life] by the adoption of a rule that he who violates that right in another forfeits it for himself."

Society Must Retain the Death Penalty for Murder, 1868

John Stuart Mill

John Stuart Mill, prominent philosopher and economist, is probably best known as the author of the famous essay, *On Liberty*. From 1865-1868 he served as a member of the British Parliament and constantly advocated political and social reforms such as emancipation for women, and the development of labor organizations and farm cooperatives. In the following viewpoint, taken from a Parliamentary Debate on April 21, 1868, Mill argues that while he is an advocate for lesser penalties for crimes such as theft, society must retain the death penalty for crimes of murder.

As you read, consider the following questions:

1. Why does the author argue that the death penalty is the most humane alternative for the criminal?
2. Does the death penalty deter crime, according to Mr. Mill?
3. Why does the author say he disagrees with the philanthropists on the issue of the death penalty?

John Stuart Mill, *Hansard's Parliamentary Debate*, 3rd Series, London: April 21, 1868.

It is always a matter of regret to me to find myself, on a public question, opposed to those who are called—sometimes in the way of honour, and sometimes in what is intended for ridicule—the philanthropists. Of all persons who take part in public affairs, they are those for whom, on the whole, I feel the greatest amount of respect; for their characteristic is, that they devote their time, their labour, and much of their money to objects purely public, with a less admixture of either personal or class selfishness, than any other class of politicians whatever. On almost all the great questions, scarcely any politicians are so steadily and almost uniformly to be found on the side of right; and they seldom err, but by an exaggerated application of some just and highly important principle. On the very subject that is now occupying us we all know what signal service they have rendered. It is through their efforts that our criminal laws . . . have so greatly relaxed their most revolting and most impolitic ferocity, that aggravated murder is now practically the only crime which is punished with death by any of our lawful tribunals; and we are even now deliberating whether the extreme penalty should be retained in that solitary case. This vast gain, not only to humanity, but to the ends of penal justice, we owe to the philanthropists; and if they are mistaken, as I cannot but think they are, in the present instance, it is only in not perceiving the right time and place for stopping in a career hitherto so eminently beneficial. Sir, there is a point at which, I conceive, that career ought to stop.

Just Penalty for Some Circumstances

When there has been brought home to any one, by conclusive evidence, the greatest crime known to the law; and when the attendant circumstances suggest no palliation of the guilt, no hope that the culprit may even yet not be unworthy to live among mankind, nothing to make it probable that the crime was an exception to his general character rather than a consequence of it, then I confess it appears to me that to deprive the criminal of the life of which he has proved himself to be unworthy—solemnly to blot him out from the fellowship of mankind and from the catalogue of the living—is the most appropriate, as it is certainly the most impressive, mode in which society can attach to so great a crime the penal consequences which for the security of life it is indispensable to annex to it. I defend this penalty, when confined to atrocious cases, on the very ground on which it is commonly attacked—on that of humanity to the criminal; as beyond comparison the least cruel mode in which it is possible adequately to deter from the crime. If, in our horror of inflicting death, we endeavour to devise some punishment for the living criminal which shall act on the human mind with a deterrent force at all comparable to that of death, we are driven to inflictions less severe indeed in appearance, and therefore less efficacious, but far more cruel in reality.

Few, I think, would venture to propose, as a punishment for aggravated murder, less than imprisonment with hard labour for life; that is the fate to which a murderer would be consigned by the mercy which shrinks from putting him to death. But has it been sufficiently considered what sort of a mercy this is, and what kind of life it leaves to him? If, indeed, the punishment is not really inflicted—if it become the sham which a few years ago such punishments were rapidly becoming—then, indeed, its adoption would be almost tantamount to giving up the attempt to repress murder altogether. But if it really is what it professes to be, and if it is realized in all its rigour by the popular imagination, as it very probably would not be, but as it must be if it is to be efficacious, it will be so shocking that when the memory of the crime is no longer fresh, there will be almost insuperable difficulty in executing it. What comparison can there really be, in point of severity, between consigning a man to the short pang of a rapid death, and immuring him in a living tomb, there to linger out what may be a long life in the hardest and most monotonous toil,

The Most Powerful Deterrent

The punishment of death is unquestionably the most powerful deterrent, the most effective preventive, that can be applied. Human nature teaches this fact. An instinct that outruns all reasoning, a dreadful horror that overcomes all other sentiments, works in us all when we contemplate it.

Samuel Hand, *The North American Review*, December 1881.

without any of its alleviations or rewards—debarred from all pleasant sights and sounds, and cut off from all earthly hope, except a slight mitigation of bodily restraint, or a small improvement of diet? Yet even such a lot as this, because there is no one moment at which the suffering is of terrifying intensity, and, above all, because it does not contain the element, so imposing to the imagination, of the unknown, is universally reputed a milder punishment than death—stands in all codes as a mitigation of the capital penalty, and is thankfully accepted as such. For it is characteristic of all punishments which depend on duration for their efficacy—all, therefore, which are not corporal or pecuniary—that they are more rigorous than they seem; while it is, on the contrary, one of the strongest recommendations a punishment can have, that it should seem more rigorous than it is; for its practical power depends far less on what it is than on what it seems.

There is not, I should think, any human infliction which makes an impression on the imagination so entirely out of proportion to its real severity as the punishment of death. The punishment must be mild indeed which does not add more to the sum of human misery than is necessarily or directly added by the execution of a criminal. . . . The most that human laws can do to anyone in the matter of death is to hasten it; the man would have died at any rate; not so very much later, and on the average, I fear, with a considerably greater amount of bodily suffering. Society is asked, then, to denude itself of an instrument of punishment which, in the grave cases to which alone it is suitable, effects its purpose at a less cost of human suffering than any other; which, while it inspires more terror, is less cruel in actual fact than any punishment that we should think of substituting for it. My hon. Friend [Mr. Gilpin] says that it does not inspire terror, and that experience proves it to be a failure. But the influence of a punishment is not to be estimated by its effect on hardened criminals. Those whose habitual way of life keeps them, so to speak, at all times within sight of the gallows, do grow to care less about it; as, to compare good things with bad, an old soldier is not much affected by the chance of dying in battle. I can afford to admit all that is often said about the indifference of professional criminals to the gallows. Though of that indifference one-third is probably bravado and another third confidence that they shall have the luck to escape, it is quite probable that the remaining third is real. But the efficacy of a punishment which acts principally through the imagination, is chiefly to be measured by the impression it makes on those who are still innocent: by the horror with which it surrounds the first promptings of guilt; the restraining influence it exercises over the beginning of the thought which, if indulged, would become a temptation; the check which it exerts over the gradual declension towards the state—never suddenly attained—in which crime no longer revolts, and punishment no longer terrifies.

Unknown Number of Lives Saved

As for what is called the failure of death punishment, who is able to judge of that? We partly know who those are whom it has not deterred; but who is there who knows whom it has deterred, or how many human beings it has saved who would have lived to be murderers if that awful association had not been thrown round the idea of murder from their earliest infancy? Let us not forget that the most imposing fact loses its power over the imagination if it is made too cheap. When a punishment fit only for the most atrocious crimes is lavished on small offences until human feeling recoils from it, then, indeed, it ceases to intimidate, because it ceases to be believed in.

The failure of capital punishment in cases of theft is easily accounted for: the thief did not believe that it would be inflicted. He had learnt by experience that jurors would perjure themselves rather than find him guilty; that Judges would seize any excuse for not sentencing him to death, or for recommending him to mercy; and that if neither jurors nor Judges were merciful, there were still hopes from an authority above both. When things had come to this pass it was high time to give up the vain attempt. When it is impossible to inflict a punishment, or when its infliction becomes a public scandal, the idle threat cannot too soon disappear from the statute book. And in the case of the host of offences which were formerly capital, I heartily rejoice that it did become impracticable to execute the law.

Deserved Retribution

Capital execution upon the deadly poisoner and the midnight assassin is not only necessary for the safety of society, it is the fit and deserved retribution of their crimes. By it alone is divine and human justice fulfilled.

Samuel Hand, *The North American Review*, December 1881.

If the same state of public feeling comes to exist in the case of murder; if the time comes when jurors refuse to find a murderer guilty; when Judges will not sentence him to death, or will recommend him to mercy; or when, if juries and Judges do not flinch from their duty, Home Secretaries, under pressure of deputations and memorials, shrink from theirs, and the threat becomes, as it became in the other cases, a mere *brutum fulmen*; then, indeed, it may become necessary to do in this case what has been done in those—to abrogate the penalty. That time may come—my hon. Friend thinks that it has nearly come. I hardly know whether he lamented it or boasted of it; but he and his Friends are entitled to the boast: for if it comes it will be their doing, and they will have gained what I cannot but call a fatal victory, for they will have achieved it by bringing about, if they will forgive me for saying so, an enervation, an effeminacy, in the general mind of the country. For what else than effeminacy is it to be so much more shocked by taking a man's life then by depriving him of all that makes life desirable or valuable? Is death, then, the greatest of all earthly ills? *Usque adeone mori miserum est?* Is it, indeed, so dreadful a thing to die? Has it not been from of old one chief part of a manly education to make us despise death—teaching us to account it, if an evil at all, by no means high in the list of evils; at all events, as an inevitable one, and to hold, as it were, our lives in our hands, ready to be given or risked at any moment, for a sufficiently worthy object? I am sure that my hon. Friends know all this as well, and have as much of all these feelings as any of the rest of us; possibly more. But I cannot think that this is likely to be the effect of their teaching on the general mind.

I cannot think that the cultivating of a peculiar sensitiveness of conscience on this one point, over and above what result from the general cultivation of the moral sentiments, is permanently consistent with assigning in our own minds to the fact of death no more than the degree of relative importance which belongs to it among the other incidents of our humanity. The men of old cared too little about death, and gave their own lives or took those of others with equal recklessness. Our danger is of the opposite kind, lest we should be so much shocked by death, in general and in the abstract, as to care too much about it in individual cases, both those of other people and our own, which call for its being risked. And I am not putting things at the worst, for it is proved by the experience of other countries that horror of the executioner by no means necessarily implies horror of the assassin. The stronghold, as we all know, of hired assassination in the 18th century was Italy; yet it is said that in some of the Italian populations the infliction of death by sentence of law was in the highest degree offensive and revolting to popular feeling. Much has been said of the sanctity of human life, and the absurdity of supposing that we can teach respect for life by ourselves destroying it. But I am surprised at the employment of this argument, for it is one which might be brought against any punishment whatever. It is not human life only, not human life as such, that ought to be sacred to us, but human feelings. The human capacity of suffering is what we should cause to be respected, not the mere capacity of existing. And we may imagine somebody asking how we can teach people not to inflict suffering by ourselves inflicting it? But to this I should answer—all of us would answer—that to deter by suffering from inflicting suffering is not only possible, but the very purpose of penal justice. Does fining a criminal show want of respect for property, or imprisoning him, for personal freedom? Just as unreasonable is it to think that to take the life of a man who has taken that of another is to show want of regard for human life. We show, on the contrary, most emphatically our regard for it, by the adoption of a rule that he who violates that right in another forfeits it for himself, and that while no other crime that he can commit deprives him of his right to live, this shall.

Mistakes Impossible to Correct

There is one argument against capital punishment, even in extreme cases, which I cannot deny to have weight . . . . It is this— that if by an error of justice an innocent person is put to death, the mistake can never be corrected; all compensation, all reparation for the wrong is impossible. This would be indeed a serious objection if these miserable mistakes—among the most tragical occurrences in the whole round of human affairs—could not be made extremely rare. The argument is invincible where the mode of criminal procedure is dangerous to the innocent, or where the Courts of Justice are not trusted. And this probably is the reason why the objection to an irreparable punishment began (as I believe it did) earlier, and is more intense and more widely diffused, in some parts of the Continent of Europe than it is here. There are on the continent great and enlightened countries, in which the criminal procedure is not so favourable to innocence, does not afford the same security against erroneous conviction, as it does among us; countries where the Courts of Justice seem to think they fail in their duty unless they find somebody guilty; and in their really laudable desire to hunt guilt from its hiding-places, expose themselves to a serious danger of condemning the innocent. If our own procedure and Courts of Justice afforded ground for similar apprehension, I should be the first to join in withdrawing the power of inflicting irreparable punishment from such tribunals. But we all know that the defects of our procedure are the very opposite.

Perish the Murderers

It is better that the murderer should perish than that innocent men and women should have their throats cut. A witty Frenchman lately wrote a pamphlet on this subject, and said—
"I am all for abolishing the penalty of death, if Messieurs the Assassins would only set the example."

Mr. Gregory, from debate before England's Parliament, April 21, 1868.

Our rules of evidence are even too favourable to the prisoner: and juries and Judges carry out the maxim, "It is better that ten guilty should escape than that one innocent person should suffer," not only to the letter, but beyond the letter. Judges are most anxious to point out, and juries to allow for, the barest possibility of the prisoner's innocence. No human judgment is infallible: such sad cases as my hon. Friend cited will sometimes occur; but in so grave a case as that of murder, the accused, in our system, has always the benefit of the merest shadow of a doubt. And this suggests another consideration very germane to the question. The very fact that death punishment is more shocking than any other to the imagination, necessarily renders the courts of Justice more scrupulous in requiring the fullest evidence of guilt. Even that which is the greatest objection to capital punishment, the impossibility of correcting an error once committed, must make, and does make, juries and Judges more careful in forming their opinion, and more jealous in their scrutiny of the evidence.

If the substitution of penal servitude for death in cases of murder should cause any relaxation in this conscientious scrupulosity, there would be a great evil to set against the real, but I hope rare, advantage of being able to make reparation to a condemned person who was afterwards discovered to be innocent. In order that the possibility of correction may be kept open wherever the chance of this sad contingency is more than infinitesimal, it is quite right that the Judge should recommend to the Crown a commutation of the sentence, not solely when the proof of guilt is open to the smallest suspicion, but whenever there remains anything unexplained and mysterious in the case, raising a desire for more light, or making it likely that further information may at some future time be obtained.

Against Total Abolition

I would also suggest that whenever the sentence is commuted the grounds of the commutation should, in some authentic form, be made known to the public. Thus much I willingly concede to my hon. Friend; but on the question of total abolition I am inclined to hope that the feeling of the country is not with him, and that the limitation of death punishment to the cases referred to in the Bill of last year will be generally considered sufficient. The mania which existed a short time ago for paring down all our punishments seems to have reached its limits, and not before it was time. We were in danger of being left without any effectual punishment, except for small offences. . . .

I think . . . that in the case of most offences, except those against property, there is more need of strengthening our punishments than of weakening them: and that severer sentences, with an apportionment of them to the different kinds of offences which shall approve itself better than at present to the moral sentiments of the community, are the kind of reform of which our penal system now stands in need.

"Putting men to death in cold blood by human law . . . . seems to me a most pernicious and brutalizing practice."

The Death Penalty Is State-Sanctioned Murder, 1872

Horace Greeley

Horace Greeley is a true American success story. Having grown up in abject poverty and with an irregular education ending at the age of 15, Greeley founded the *New York Tribune* in 1841 and made it one of the most influential papers in the country. A social reformer, he was one of the first to implement profit sharing—a system in which employees share in the profits of a company. Other reforms advocated by Greeley were temperance, women's rights, and a homestead law. He ran for president against Ulysses S. Grant in 1872 and lost. The combination of the loss of the election and the death of his wife a few days before resulted in his insanity and death on November 29, 1872. In the following viewpoint Greeley addresses four points he believes prove the death penalty is dangerous and brutal.

As you read, consider the following questions:

1. Why does the author argue the death penalty is now obsolete?
2. Why does Mr. Greeley believe the death penalty sanctions revenge?

Horace Greeley, *Hints Toward Reforms in Lectures, Addresses and Other Writings*. New York: Harper & Brothers, 1850.

Is it ever justifiable . . . to [kill] malefactors by sentence of law? I answer Yes, *provided* Society can in no other way be secured against a repetition of the culprit's offence. In committing a murder, for instance, he has proved himself capable of committing more murders—perhaps many. The possibility of a thousand murders is developed in his one act of felonious homicide. Call his moral state depravity, insanity, or whatever you please, he is manifestly a ferocious, dangerous animal, who can not safely be permitted to go at large. Society must be secured against the reasonable probability of his killing others, and, where that can only be effected by taking his life, his life must be taken.

—But suppose him to be in New-England, New-York or Pennsylvania—arrested, secured and convicted—Society's rebel, outcast and prisoner of war—taken with arms in his hands. Here are prison-cells wherefrom escape is impossible; and if there be any fear of his assaulting his keeper or others, that may be most effectively prevented. Is it expedient or salutary to crush the life out of this helpless, abject, pitiable wretch?

A Sorrowful Mistake

I for one think it decidedly *is not*—that it is a sorrowful mistake and barbarity to do any such thing. In saying this, I do not assume to decide whether Hanging or Imprisonment for Life is the severer penalty. I should wish to understand clearly the moral state of the prisoner before I attempted to guess; and, even then, I know too little of the scenes of untried being which lie next beyond the confines of this mortal existence to say whether it were better for any penitent or hardened culprit to be hung next month or left in prison to die a natural death. What is best for that culprit I leave to God, who knows when is the fit time for him to die. My concern is with Society—the moral it teaches, the conduct it tacitly enjoins. And I feel that the choking to death of this culprit works harm, in these respects, namely:

1. *It teaches and sanctions Revenge.* There is a natural inclination in man to return injury for injury, evil for evil. It is the exciting cause of many murders as well as less flagrant crimes. It stands in no need of stimulation—its prompt repression at all times is one of the chief trials even of good men. But A.B. has committed a murder, is convicted of and finally hung for it. Bill, Dick and Jim, three apprentices of ordinary understanding and attainments, beg away or run away to witness the hanging. Ask either of them, 'What is this man hung for?' and the prompt, correct answer will be, 'Because he killed C.D.'—not 'To prevent his killing others,' nor yet 'To prevent others from killing.' Well: the three enjoy the spectacle and turn away satisfied. On their way home, a scuffle is commenced in fun, but gradually changes to a fight, wherein one finds himself down with two holding and

beating him. Though sorely exasperated and severely suffering, he can not throw them off, but he can reach with one hand the knife in his vest pocket. Do you fancy he will be more or less likely to use it because of that moral spectacle which Society has just proffered for his delectation and improvement? You may say Less if you can, but I say More! many times more! You may preach to him that Revenge is right for Society but wrong for him till your head is gray, and he perhaps may listen to you—but not till after he has opened his knife and made a lunge with it.

Murder an Abhorrent Crime

2. *It tends to weaken and destroy the natural horror of bloodshed.* Man has a natural horror of taking the life of his fellow man. His instincts revolt at it—his conscience condemns it—his frame shudders at the thought of it. But let him see first one and then another strung up between heaven and earth and choked to death, with due formalities of Law and solemnities of Religion—the slayer not accounted an evil-doer but an executor of the State's just decree, a pillar of the Social edifice—and his horror of bloodshed *per se* sensibly and rapidly oozes away, and he comes to look at killing men as quite the thing provided there be adequate reason for it.

Death Penalty Unnecessary

It is not necessary to hang the murderer in order to guard society against him, and to prevent him from repeating the crime. If it were, we should hang the maniac, who is the most dangerous murderer. Society may defend itself by other means than by destroying life. Massachusetts can build prisons strong enough to secure the community forever against convicted felons.

Robert Rantoul Jr., *Report to the Legislature,* 1836.

But what reason? and whose? The law slays the slayer; but in his sight the corrupter or calumniator of his wife or sister, the traducer of his character, the fraudulent bankrupt who has involved and ruined his friend, is every whit as great a villain as the man-slayer, and deserving of as severe a punishment. Yet the Law makes no provision for such punishment—hardly for any punishment at all—and what shall he do? He can not consent that the guilty go 'unwhipt of justice,' so he takes his rifle and deals out full measure of it. He is but doing as Society has taught him by example. War, dueling, bloody affrays, &c., find their nourishment and support in the Gallows.

3. *It facilitates and often insures the escape of the guilty from any punishment by human law.*—Jurors (whether for or against Capital Punishment) dread to convict where the crime is Death. Human

judgment is fallible; human testimony may mislead. Witnesses often lie—sometimes conspire to lie plausibly and effectively. Circumstances often strongly point to a conclusion which is after all a false one. The real murderers sometimes conspire to fasten suspicion on some innocent person, and so arrange the circumstances that he can hardly escape their toils. Sometimes they appear in court as witnesses against him, and swear the crime directly upon him. A single legal work contains a list of one hundred cases in which men were hung for crimes which they were afterward proved entirely innocent of. And for every such case there have doubtless been many wherein juries, unwilling to take life where there was a *possibility* of innocence, have given the prisoner the benefit of a very faint doubt and acquitted him. Had the penalty been Imprisonment, they would have convicted, notwithstanding the bare possibility of his innocence, since any future developments in his favor, through the retraction of witnesses, the clearing up of circumstances, or the confession of the actual culprit, would at once lead to his liberation and to an earnest effort by the community to repay him for his unmerited ignominy and suffering. But choke the prisoner to death, and any development in his favor is thenceforth too late. Next year may prove him innocent beyond cavil nor doubt; but of what avail is that to the victim over whose grave the young grass is growing? And thus, through the inexorable character of the Death-Penalty, hundreds of the innocent suffer an undeserved and ignominious death, while tens of thousands of the guilty escape any punishment by human law.

Sympathizing with the Criminal

4. *It excites a pernicious sympathy for the convict.*—We ought ever to be merciful toward the sinful and guilty, remembering our own misdeeds and imperfections. We ought to regard with a benignant compassion those whom Crime has doomed to suffer. But the criminal is not a hero, nor a martyr, and should not be made to resemble one. A crowd of ten to fifty thousand persons, witnessing the infliction of the law's just penalty on an offender, and half of them sobbing and crying from sympathy for his fate, is not a wholesome spectacle—far otherwise. The impression it makes is not that of the majesty and Divine benignity of Law—the sovereignty and beneficence of Justice. Thousands are hoping, praying, entreating that a pardon may yet come—some will accuse the Executive of cruelty and hardness of heart in withholding it. While this furnace of sighs is at red heat, this tempest of sobs in full career, the culprit is swung off—a few faint; many shudder; more feel an acute shock of pain; while the great mass adjourn to take a general drink, some of them swearing that *this* hanging was a great shame—that the man did not really deserve it. Do you fancy the greater number have imbibed and will profit by the

intended lesson?

—But I do not care to pile argument on argument, consideration on consideration, in opposition to the expediency, in this day and section, of putting men to death in cold blood by human law. It seems to me a most pernicious and brutalizing practice. Indeed, the recent enactments of our own, with most if not all of the Free States, whereby Executions are henceforth to take place in private, or in the presence of a few select witnesses only, seem clearly to admit the fact. They certainly imply that Executions are of no use

Capital Punishment

Paul Conrad, © 1985, Los Angeles Times, Reprinted with Permission.

as examples—that they rather tend to make criminals than to reform those already depraved. When I see any business or vocation sneaking and skulking in dark lanes and little by-streets which elude observation, I conclude that those who follow such business feel at least doubtful of its utility and beneficence. They may *argue* that it is 'a necessary evil,' but they can hardly put faith in their own logic. When I see the bright array of many-colored liquor bottles, which formerly filled flauntingly the post of honor in every tip-top hotel, now hustled away into some sideroom, and finally down into a dark basement, out of the sight and knowledge of all but those who especially seek them, I say exultingly, 'Good for so much! one more 'hoist, and they will be—where they should be—out of sight 'and reach altogether:'—so, when I see the Gallows, once the denizen of some swelling eminence, the cynosure of ten thousand eyes, 'the observed of all observers,' skulking and hiding itself from public view in jail-yards, shutting itself up in prisons, I say, 'You have taken the right road! Go 'ahead! One more drive, and your detested, rickety frame 'is out of the sight of civilized man for ever!'

*"It is the finality of the death penalty
which instils fear into the heart of every
murderer, and it is this fear of punishment
which protects society."*

Capital Punishment Is a Safeguard for Society, 1925

Robert E. Crowe

In early 1925 when Judge Robert E. Crowe wrote his opinion of the death penalty, he was State's Attorney for Cook County, Illinois. He had just been the prosecutor in the widely publicized trial of Leopold and Loeb, two young men who were charged with the thrill-murder of a young boy. The first World War had not been over for long and America was beginning to focus again on its own growing problem of crime. In this viewpoint Judge Crowe defends the American legal system and the necessity of ridding society of murderers in order to secure safety for its members and deter further murders.

As you read, consider the following questions:

1. Why does the author believe that a murderer is a danger to all of society?
2. How does Judge Crowe think the American system protects the accused criminal?
3. What arguments does the author offer for his statement that capital punishment is a deterrent to crime?

Robert E. Crowe, "Capital Punishment Protects Society," *The Forum*, February 1925.

I believe that the penalty for murder should be death. I urge capital punishment for murder not because I believe that society wishes to take the life of a murderer but because society does not wish to lose its own. I advocate this extreme and irrevocable penalty because the punishment is commensurate with the crime. The records, I believe, will show that the certainty of punishment is a deterrent of crime. As the law is written in most of the States of the Union, every other form of punishment is revocable at the will of an individual.

It is the finality of the death penalty which instils fear into the heart of every murderer, and it is this fear of punishment which protects society. Murderers are not punished for revenge. The man with the life blood of another upon his hands is a menace to the life of every citizen. He should be removed from society for the sake of society. In his removal, society is sufficiently protected, but only provided it is a permanent removal. I should like to see the experiment of the inexorable infliction of the death penalty upon all deliberate murderers tried out in every State of the Union for a sufficient period of time to demonstrate whether or not it is the most effective and most certain means of checking the appalling slaughter of innocent, peaceful, and law-abiding citizens which has gone on without check for so many years, and which is increasing at a rate which has won for the United States of America the disgrace of being known as "the most lawless nation claiming place among the civilized nations of the world."

Duty to Society

The attitude which society must take toward offenders,—great as well as small,—must not be confused with the attitude which the individual quite properly may assume. Neither may officers of the law nor leaders of public thought, if they are mindful of the duty which they owe to society, advocate a substitution of any other penalty for murder than that penalty which will give to society the greatest degree of protection. . . .

In cases where,—in a properly constituted court over whose deliberations a properly elected or appointed judge has presided and in which, after hours and days and sometimes weeks of patient and deliberate inquiry, a jury of twelve men selected in the manner which the law provides,—a man charged with murder has been found guilty and sentenced to death, it is an unpardonable abuse of the great power of executive clemency to nullify the verdict by commuting the sentence to life imprisonment. It is in effect a usurpation by the executive authority of the state of powers and duties deliberately and expressly assigned by the representatives of the people in the constitution to the judicial branch alone.

I not believe that the American Bar is ready to plead guilty to the charge which this action infers that lawyers for the prosecution and lawyers for the defense are so venal, corrupt, and bloodthirsty through ulterior motives as to deliberately conspire with an unrighteous judge, an unprincipled or irresponsible jury and witnesses prompted solely by the spirit of revenge to doom to death any man on a charge of murder unless the testimony truly shows him guilty beyond all reasonable doubt. . . .

Faith in Americans

It is because of my faith and trust in the integrity of our American citizens that I believe that there is no considerable danger that the innocent man will be convicted and that society may be charged that in a blind zeal to protect itself against murder it actually commits murder by the infliction of the death penalty.

The man who kills is society's greatest enemy. He has set up his own law. He is an anarchist,—the foe of all civilized government. If anarchy is not to be met with anarchy, it must be met by the laws, and these laws must be enforced. . . .

Penalize Offenders

If we want order, we must stop being soft-headed sentimentalists when it comes to penalizing offenders. The murder rate in the United States rises to a scandalous figure. Of the many who kill, comparatively few are ever arrested, still fewer convicted, fewer yet ever see the inside of a felon's cell; only rarely is the murderer punished as the law says he shall be. A life term is commonly a short vacation at State expense with nothing to do but eat the fruit of others' industry. Americans are not a nation of murder lovers. We merely seem to be. We are made to seem to be by ill-prepared judges, woozy jurors, and a public opinion sentimentally inclined to sympathize more with the perpetrators than the victims of major crimes. This country needs a rededication to the everlasting truth that the fear of prompt and adequate punishment is the best deterrent for gentlemen tempted to slay. This violates long book-shelves of theory.

Editorial, *Cleveland Plain Dealer*, January 25, 1925.

Why are there so few violations of the laws of the United States? When a man files his income tax schedule, why does he hire an auditor to see that he makes no mistake, and why does the same man when he goes before our Boards of Assessors and Boards of Review and schedules his personal property for taxation in Chicago as well as elsewhere conceal millions upon which he should be taxed? Why? Because when you get into the United States court after having violated the laws of the United States, if you are guilty, no plea of mercy, however eloquent or by whomsoever delivered, will cheat the law there.

We hear much about England. There murder is murder. Justice

is swift and sure. There are fewer murders in the entire Kingdom of Great Britain yearly than there are in the city of Chicago.

In recent years the American public has been influenced to some extent by an active, persistent, and systematic agitation based upon an unfortunate and misplaced sympathy for persons accused of crime. I say unfortunate and misplaced sympathy because it is a sympathy guided by emotion and impulse rather than upon reason and compassion for the prisoners at the bar. It is so deep and soul stirring that it loses its sense of proportion. It forgets the life that was blotted out. It forgets the broken-hearted left behind. It forgets the fatherless and sometimes homeless children which should be the real object of pity. It forgets that they become charges upon the state and it also forgets that there has been established a broken home,—the one in the group of homes from which twice as many criminals come as from those which remain intact.

Opponents of capital punishment think somewhat along the same lines. They forget that murder is inexorable and that the victim never returns. They forget that society is protected best by punishment which is proportionate to the crime. They are moved to abolish hanging because it is an unwholesome spectacle. They overlook the unwholesome and harrowing aspects of a murder scene.

Some who admit the justice of capital punishment deny its necessity. They argue that in taking the life of an offender society is wreaking vengeance upon a helpless individual, while, as a matter of fact, the exact opposite is true. If an individual were to slay another who was guilty of murder, especially if he had no fear of him, the act would be prompted by revenge. And when we realize that many of our present-day murderers are professional criminals whose victims were slain in the course of holdups, robberies, and other crimes committed for profit, and that the victim was killed deliberately on the theory that dead men can make no identifications, we know at once that they did not kill for revenge and that they had no malice against the individual they killed. Society for its own protection should make it impossible for these men to kill again.

Crime Against Society

Murder like all other crime is a crime against society. It is for assault upon society that the state inflicts punishment. Too many confuse the relation of the victim of a crime with that of the interest of the state in the prosecution of criminals. The state is impersonal. It is the voice for all of the people expressed by a voting majority. What happens or has happened to any individual is not of great importance. The civil courts exist for the adjudication of the individual and personal wrong. The criminal court exists to

46

punish those who have offended against the state. He who violates the criminal code offends against and injures us all. When he injures to the extent of unlawfully taking human life, he has committed a grave and irreparable injury.

Punishment of the slayer will not bring back life to the victim. But punishment for crime is not inflicted upon any theory of relationship to the victim except to consider the fact that the victim was a part of society and that in wronging the individual that society itself has been assaulted.

Responsibility for Actions

I am not ready to agree to the theory that all or most murderers are not responsible for their acts. I believe that man is entitled to free will and that except in rare instances he is both morally and legally responsible for all his acts. I cannot accept the theory that murderers should not be punished for their crime because they are irresponsible. If they are so irresponsible as to constitute a danger to society, I do not believe that society can carefully preserve in existence the danger they represent. I believe that society is justified in destroying even the irresponsible murderer if he is known to imperil the life of other persons. There should be no sentiment about it. Persons whose existence means death and disaster to others who have done no wrong have no claim upon society for anything,—not even for life itself.

Safety of Citizens

Nothing is more remarkable in the evolution of a community than the growing regard for human life. A community is held to be civilized, or not, in exact proportion to the safety of the common citizen. When the life of an individual is unjustly taken by another individual, the horror of the community for such an act cannot be adequately and proportionately manifested except as the community surmounts sentiment and exacts the life of the killer in payment—after a trial, where all opportunity of defense is accorded, and after all possible human excuses and palliations have been alleged, tested, and found insufficient.

R.L. Calder, "Is Capital Punishment Right? A Debate,"*The Forum*, September 1928.

Few men who murder have previously lived blameless lives. The act of murder is the climax,—a cumulative effect of countless previous thoughts and acts. The man's conduct depends upon his philosophy of life. Those who want to grow up to be respectable and useful citizens in the community have a correct philosophy. Those who want to excel in crime, those who tear down instead of building up, deliberately choose to adopt the wrong philosophy of life and to make their conduct correspond with it.

Society and particularly the state would not be much concerned with individual codes of conduct if, at the present time, they were not adopted by the youths of the land and were not creating an army of virtual anarchists who look upon the criminal code, including that part of it forbidding murder, as a mere convention of society which "advanced thinking" and crazy social theories permit them to set aside as a matter of no consequence.

Because some of the youth of our population are saturated with these ideas, we are asked to accept fantastic notions, abnormal actions, and even defiance, disregard, and violation of the law, as the reason for turning them loose when charged with murder. We are compelled to listen to the weirdest, wildest, and most fantastic theories expounded by expert witnesses to show why capital punishment should not be inflicted. . . .

If the United States of America has the power to take boys of eighteen years of age and send them to their death in the front line trenches in countries overseas in defense of our laws, I believe that the state has an equal right to take the lives of murderers of like age for violating the mandate of God and man, "Thou shalt not kill."

Deterrent of Crime

I base my belief that capital punishment is a deterrent of crime upon the fact that where capital punishment has been inflicted for even a comparatively small period and in a relatively small number of cases, there subsequently has been an immediate decrease in murder. Those who argue against capital punishment should bear in mind that where capital punishment has actually been inflicted, this has been the result. But, capital punishment has never been given a fair trial throughout this country over a sufficient period of time and in a sufficient number of cases to justify the assumption that it is not a deterrent of murder.

Until American society finds a way to protect itself from the murder of its members, this country will continue to be known as "the most lawless nation claiming place among the civilized nations of the world." I am not proud of that appellation. I hang my head in shame whenever I hear it. I believe society should have no hesitancy in springing the trap every time the noose can be put around a murderer's neck.

"It is hardly probable that the great majority of people refrain from killing their neighbors because they are afraid; they refrain because they never had the inclination."

Capital Punishment Will Not Safeguard Society, 1928

Clarence Darrow

Clarence Darrow was a Chicago lawyer who became famous for his handling of criminal and labor cases. He chose to defend those whom he considered social unfortunates. He argued in behalf of over 100 people charged with murder, none of whom were sentenced to death. Although he retired in 1927, he continued to write prolifically on the causes of crime and to argue vehemently for the abolition of the death penalty. His most famous courtroom pleas are included in the book, *Attorney for the Damned*. In the following viewpoint, Mr. Darrow maintains that capital punishment is no deterrent to crime. He advances his theory that as victims of their culture, criminals need to be treated more humanely.

As you read, consider the following questions:

1. To what does Mr. Darrow attribute the causes of crime, specifically murder?
2. What arguments does the author offer to support his belief that capital punishment is no deterrent for murder?

Clarence Darrow, "The Futility of the Death Penalty," *The Forum*, September 1928.

Little more than a century ago, in England, there were over two hundred offenses that were punishable with death. The death sentence was passed upon children under ten years old. And every time the sentimentalist sought to lessen the number of crimes punishable by death, the self-righteous said no, that it would be the destruction of the state; that it would be better to kill for more transgressions rather than for less.

Today, both in England and America, the number of capital offenses has been reduced to a very few, and capital punishment would doubtless be abolished altogether were it not for the self-righteous, who still defend it with the same old arguments. Their major claim is that capital punishment decreases the number of murders, and hence, that the state must retain the institution as its last defense against the criminal.

It is my purpose in this article to prove, first, that capital punishment is no deterrent to crime; and second, that the state continues to kill its victims, not so much to defend society against them—for it could do that equally well by imprisonment—but to appease the mob's emotions of hatred and revenge.

The Criminal Disease

Behind the idea of capital punishment lies false training and crude views of human conduct. People do evil things, say the judges, lawyers, and preachers, because of depraved hearts. Human conduct is not determined by the causes which determine the conduct of other animal and plant life in the universe. For some mysterious reason human beings act as they please; and if they do not please to act in a certain way, it is because, having the power of choice, they deliberately choose to act wrongly. The world once applied this doctrine to disease and insanity in men. It was also applied to animals, and even inanimate things were once tried and condemned to destruction. The world knows better now, but the rule has not yet been extended to human beings.

The simple fact is that every person starts life with a certain physical structure, more or less sensitive, stronger or weaker. He is played upon by everything that reaches him from without, and in this he is like everything else in the universe, inorganic matter as well as organic. How a man will act depends upon the character of his human machine, and the strength of the various stimuli that affect it. Everyone knows that this is so in disease and insanity. Most investigators know that it applies to crime. But the great mass of people still sit in judgment, robed with self-righteousness, and determine the fate of their less fortunate fellows. When this question is studied like any other, we shall then know how to get rid of most of the conduct that we call "criminal," just as we are now getting rid of much of the disease that once afflicted mankind.

If crime were really the result of willful depravity, we should

50

be ready to concede that capital punishment may serve as a deterrent to the criminally inclined. But it is hardly probable that the great majority of people refrain from killing their neighbors because they are afraid; they refrain because they never had the inclination. Human beings are creatures of habit and, as a rule, they are not in the habit of killing. The circumstances that lead to killings are manifold, but in a particular individual the inducing cause is not easily found. In one case, homicide may have been induced by indigestion in the killer; in another, it may be traceable to some weakness inherited from a remote ancestor; but that it results from *something* tangible and understandable, if all the facts were known, must be plain to everyone who believes in cause and effect.

Punishment No Cure for Crime

There is no deterrent in the menace of the gallows.

Cruelty and viciousness are not abolished by cruelty and viciousness—not even by legalized cruelty and viciousness . . . .

Our penal system has broken down because it is built upon the sand—founded on the basis of force and violence—instead of on the basis of Christian care of our fellow men, of moral and mental human development, of the conscientious performance by the State of its duty to the citizen.

We cannot cure murder by murder.

We must adopt another and better system.

William Randolph Hearst, *The Congressional Digest*, August-September 1927.

Of course, no one will be converted to this point of view by statistics of crime. In the first place, it is impossible to obtain reliable ones; and in the second place, the conditions to which they apply are never the same. But if one cares to analyze the figures, such as we have, it is easy to trace the more frequent causes of homicide. The greatest number of killings occur during attempted burglaries and robberies. The robber knows that penalties for burglary do not average more than five years in prison. He also knows that the penalty for murder is death or life imprisonment. Faced with this alternative, what does the burglar do when he is detected and threatened with arrest? He shoots to kill. He deliberately takes the chance of death to save himself from a five-year term in prison. It is therefore as obvious as anything can be that fear of death has no effect in diminishing homicides of this kind, which are more numerous than any other type.

The next largest number of homicides may be classed as "sex

murders." Quarrels between husbands and wives, disappointed love, or love too much requited cause many killings. They are the result of primal emotions so deep that the fear of death has not the slightest effect in preventing them. Spontaneous feelings overflow in criminal acts, and consequences do not count. Then there are cases of sudden anger, uncontrollable rage. The fear of death never enters into such cases; if the anger is strong enough, consequences are not considered until too late. The old-fashioned stories of men deliberately plotting and committing murder in cold blood have little foundation in real life. Such killings are so rare that they need not concern us here. The point to be emphasized is that practically all homicides are manifestations of well-recognized human emotions, and it is perfectly plain that the fear of excessive punishment does not enter into them.

In addition to these personal forces which overwhelm weak men and lead them to commit murder, there are also many social and economic forces which must be listed among the causes of homicides, and human beings have even less control over these than over their own emotions. It is often said that in America there are more homicides in proportion to population than in England. This is true. There are likewise more in the United States than in Canada. But such comparisons are meaningless until one takes into consideration the social and economic differences in the countries compared. Then it becomes apparent why the homicide rate in the United States is higher. Canada's population is largely rural; that of the United States is crowded into cities whose slums are the natural breeding places of crime. Moreover, the population of England and Canada is homogeneous, while the United States has gathered together people of every color from every nation in the world. Racial differences intensify social, religious, and industrial problems, and the confusion which attends this indiscriminate mixing of races and nationalities is one of the most fertile sources of crime.

Primitive Beliefs

Will capital punishment remedy these conditions? Of course it won't; but its advocates argue that the fear of this extreme penalty will hold the victims of adverse conditions in check. To this piece of sophistry the continuance and increase of crime in our large cities is a sufficient answer. No, the plea that capital punishment acts as a deterrent to crime will not stand. The real reason why this barbarous practice persists in a so-called civilized world is that people still hold the primitive belief that the taking of one human life can be atoned for by taking another. It is the age-old obsession with punishment that keeps the official headsman busy plying his trade.

And it is precisely upon this point that I would build my case against capital punishment. Even if one grants that the idea of

52

punishment is sound, crime calls for something more—for careful study, for an understanding of causes, for proper remedies. To attempt to abolish crime by killing the criminal is the easy and foolish way out of a serious situation. Unless a remedy deals with the conditions which foster crime, criminals will breed faster than the hangman can spring his trap. Capital punishment ignores the causes of crime just as completely as the primitive witch doctor ignored the causes of disease; and, like the methods of the witch doctor, it is not only ineffective as a remedy, but is positively vicious in at least two ways. In the first place, the spectacle of state executions feeds the basest passions of the mob. And in the second place, so long as the state rests content to deal with crime in this barbaric and futile manner, society will be lulled by a false sense of security, and effective methods of dealing with crime will be discouraged. . . .

Crime in England

For the last five or six years, in England and Wales, the homicides reported by the police range from sixty-five to seventy a year. Death sentences meted out by jurors have averaged about thirty-five, and hangings, fifteen. More than half of those convicted by juries were saved by appeals to the Home Office. But in America there is no such percentage of lives saved after conviction. Governors are afraid to grant clemency. If they did, the newspapers and the populace would refuse to reelect them.

Failure to Instill Fear

It is a fact that a large percentage of murders are committed in the heat of passion, when the murderer is not in a position to reason; fear of the law plays no part at all. In the remaining few, whatever fear there may be is more than balanced by the belief on the part of the criminal that he is not going to get caught. There are also some who deliberately kill; but the knowledge that they will be caught and punished does not deter them.

Thomas Mott Osborne, "Thou Shalt Not Kill," *The Forum*, February 1925.

It is true that trials are somewhat prompter in England than America, but there no newspaper dares publish the details of any case until after the trial. In America the accused is often convicted by the public within twenty-four hours of the time a homicide occurs. The courts sidetrack all other business so that a homicide that is widely discussed may receive prompt attention. The road to the gallows is not only opened but greased for the opportunity of killing another victim. . . .

Human conduct is by no means so simple as our moralists have led us to believe. There is no sharp line separating good actions from bad. The greed for money, the display of wealth, the despair of those who witness the display, the poverty, oppression, and hopelessness of the unfortunate—all these are factors which enter into human conduct and of which the world takes no account. Many people have learned no other profession but robbery and burglary. The processions moving steadily through our prisons to the gallows are in the main made up of these unfortunates. And how do we dare to consider ourselves civilized creatures when, ignoring the causes of crime, we rest content to mete our harsh punishments to the victims of conditions over which they have no control?

Even now, are not all imaginative and humane people shocked at the spectacle of a killing by the state? How many men and women would be willing to act as executioners? How many fathers and mothers would want their children to witness an official kill-ing? What kind of people read the sensational reports of an ex-ecution? If all right-thinking men and women were not ashamed of it, why would it be needful that judges and lawyers and preachers apologize for the barbarity? How can the state censure the cruelty of the man who—moved by strong passions, or acting to save his freedom, or influenced by weakness or fear—takes human life, when everyone knows that the state itself, after long premeditation and settled hatred, not only kills, but first tortures and bedevils its victims for weeks with the impending doom?

More Humane Criminal Code

For the last hundred years the world has shown a gradual tendency to mitigate punishment. We are slowly learning that this way of controlling human beings is both cruel and ineffective. In England the criminal code has consistently grown more humane, until now the offenses punishable by death are reduced to prac-tically one. If there is any reason for singling out this one, neither facts nor philopsphy can possibly demonstrate it. There is no doubt whatever that the world is growing more humane and more sen-sitive and more understanding. The time will come when all peo-ple will view with horror the light way in which society and its courts of law now take human life; and when that time comes, the way will be clear to devise some better method of dealing with poverty and ignorance and their frequent by-products which we call crime.

Understanding Words in Context

Readers occasionally come across words which they do not recognize. And frequently, because they do not know a word or words, they will not fully understand the passage being read. Obviously, the reader can look up an unfamiliar word in a dictionary. However, by carefully examining the word in the context in which it is used, the word's meaning can often be determined. A careful reader may find clues to the meaning of the word in surrounding words, ideas, and attitudes.

Below are sentences adapted from the viewpoints in this chapter. In each excerpt, one or two words are printed in italics. Try to determine the meaning of each word by reading the excerpt. Under each excerpt you will find four definitions for the italicized word. Choose the one that is closest to your understanding of the word.

Finally, use a dictionary to see how well you have understood the words in context. It will be helpful to discuss with others the clues which helped you decide on each word's meaning.

1. Since bad men are grown so much more *INCORRIGIBLE* than in our forefathers' days, is it not fit that good men should grow less merciful to them since gentler methods are *INEFFECTUAL*?

   INCORRIGIBLE means:
   a) merciful   c) beyond reform
   b) lazy   d) violent

   INEFFECTUAL means:
   a) ineffective   c) worthwhile
   b) more powerful   d) unjust

2. If death be due to a man who *SURREPTITIOUSLY* steals the value of five shillings, surely he who puts me in fear of my life deserves another sort of *CENSURE*; he deserves to feel himself die.

SURREPTITIOUSLY means:
a) unfortunately
b) sneakily
c) viciously
d) evilly

CENSURE means:
a) death
b) guilt
c) reward
d) disapproval

3. The laws are only the sum of the smallest portions of the private liberty of each individual, and represent the general will, which is the *AGGREGATE* of that of each individual.

AGGREGATE means:
a) symbol
b) achievement
c) combination
d) justice

4. The death of a criminal is a terrible but momentary spectacle, and therefore a less *EFFICACIOUS* method of deterring others than the continued example of a man deprived of his liberty.

EFFICACIOUS means:
a) terrible
b) common
c) lasting
d) effective

5. Opponents of capital punishment forget that murder is *INEXORABLE* and that the victim never returns.

INEXORABLE means:
a) unforgivable
b) unchangeable
c) tragic
d) unjust

6. Until American society finds a way to protect itself from the murder of its members, this country will continue to be known as "the most lawless nation claiming place among the civilized nations of the world." I am not proud of that *APPELLATION*.

APPELLATION means:
a) ghost
b) mountain chain in the Eastern United States
c) name
d) foreign reputation

7. Advocates of capital punishment argue that the fear of this extreme penalty will eliminate crime. To this piece of *SOPHISTRY* the continuance and increase of crime in our large cities is a sufficient answer.

SOPHISTRY means:
a) foolishness
b) fear
c) wisdom
d) truth

Is the Death Penalty Immoral?

"[Capital punishment] expresses the extreme disapproval of the community by imposing its most extreme punishment."

The Death Penalty Is Moral

Ernest van den Haag

Ernest van den Haag is the John M. Olin Professor of Jurisprudence and Public Policy at Fordham University and a Distinguished Scholar at the Heritage Foundation. He is the author of *Punishing Criminals* and has contributed chapters to over forty books as well as innumerable articles for such diverse publications as *The New York Times, Harper's,* the *Atlantic Monthly, Esquire, Psychology Today, Fortune,* and *National Review.* In the following viewpoint, Mr. van den Haag states why he believes that the death penalty serves society as deserved retribution for the crime of murder.

As you read, consider the following questions:

1. According to the author, how does the death penalty as retributive justice differ from personal revenge?
2. Why does the author believe that punishment rather than rehabilitation is the moral prescription for wrongdoings?
3. In Mr. van den Haag's opinion, how is the "sanctity of life" defended by the use of the death penalty?

Ernest van den Haag and John P. Conrad, *The Death Penalty: A Debate.* New York: Plenum Publishing Corporation, 1983. Reprinted with permission.

It has frequently been argued that capital punishment is imposed merely to gratify an unworthy desire for revenge—unchristian, uncharitable, and futile. Is it? And is revenge the reason for capital punishment? Obviously capital punishment is imposed not only for revenge or retribution, but also for the sake of deterrence—to spare future victims of murder by carrying out the threat of execution upon convicted murderers. But let me leave this aside for the moment.

Revenge and Retribution

Retribution certainly does play a role. It differs from revenge in some respects, though not in all. Revenge is a private matter, a wish to "get even" with a person one feels has injured one, whether or not what the person did was legal. Unlike revenge, retribution is legally threatened beforehand for an act prohibited by law. It is imposed by due process and only for a crime, as threatened by law. Retribution is also limited by law. Retribution may be exacted when there is no personal injury and no wish for revenge; conversely, revenge may be carried out when there was neither a crime nor a real injury. The desire for revenge is a personal feeling. Retribution is a legally imposed social institution.

Nonetheless, the motives socialized by punishment, including the death penalty, may well include the motive of revenge. But motives should not be confused with purposes, and least of all with effects. The motive for, say, capital punishment may well be revenge, at least on the part of the father bereaved by the murder of his daughter. The intention of the law, however, may be to deter other murderers or to strengthen social solidarity by retributive punishment. Either or both or neither of these effects may be achieved.

Consider now the motive of revenge. Is it so contemptible after all? Perhaps forgiveness is better. It does not follow that revenge is bad. It can be, after all, a compensatory and psychologically reparative act. I cannot see wherein revenge must be morally blameworthy if the injury for which vengeance is exacted is. However, revenge may be socially disruptive: Only the avenger determines what to avenge, on whom, to what degree, when, and for what. This leaves far too much room for the arbitrary infliction of harm. Therefore, societies always have tried to limit and regulate revenge by transforming it into legal retribution, by doing justice according to what is deserved in place of the injured party.

Retribution is hard to define. It is harder still to determine the punishments that should be exacted by "just deserts" once the *lex talionis* is abandoned. Yet retribution does give the feeling of justice that is indispensable if the law is to be socially supported. In the case of murder, there is not much doubt about the penalty demanded by our sense of justice. It is hard to see why the law

59

should promise a murderer that what he did to his victim will never be done to him, that he will be supported and protected in prison as long as he lives, at taxpayers' expense.

Trendy Churchmen

Although trendy churchmen recently have tended to deny it, historically the main Christian churches, Roman Catholic and Protestant, have staunchly supported the death penalty, often on the basis of numerous biblical passages advocating it for murder and sometimes for transgressions that today we regard as minor. The oft-quoted "vengeance is mine, I will repay, saith the Lord" (Rom. 12:19) is not as opposed to vengeance as it is made to appear. Paul does not quote the Lord as rejecting vengeance but as reserving it to himself: You must not seek vengeance, you must leave it to the Lord. According to Christian tradition, the punishments the Lord will inflict upon those whom he does not forgive are far more terrible and lasting than what any vengeful mortal could inflict on another. What could be worse than hell, the punishment inflicted for violating God's law? God recognizes and does not deprecate the desire for vengeance. He tells us to leave the fulfillment of this desire to Him.

If we return to earth and read on after Romans 12, we find in the next chapter, 13, what the Apostle Paul actually had in mind. "The Ruler," he says in 13:4, "beareth not the sword in vain: for he is the minister of God, a revenger to execute wrath upon him that doeth evil." The meaning is clear. The Ruler, not the injured individual, should "execute wrath." Disruptive private vengeance should be institutionalized and replaced by social retribution, retribution by the ruler. . . .

Retribution Serves Social Justice

Capital punishment is an expression of society's moral outrage at particularly offensive conduct. This function may be unappealing to many, but it is essential in an ordered society that asks its citizens to rely on legal processes rather than self-help to vindicate their wrongs. . . .

Indeed, the decision that capital punishment may be the appropriate sanction in extreme cases is an expression of the community's belief that certain crimes are themselves so grievous an affront to humanity that the only adequate response may be the penalty of death.

Joel M. Gora, *Due Process of Law*, 1979.

If offenders are to suffer the punishments deserved by their crimes, if punishments are to proclaim the blame the community attaches to their crimes, capital punishment certainly accomplishes as much. It expresses the extreme disapproval of the community by imposing its most extreme punishment. Of the four ends punishment may accomplish—retribution, rehabilitation, incapacitation, and deterrence—capital punishment accomplishes three, more thoroughly than any other punishment can, while making rehabilitation irrelevant. . . .

Morally, I do not believe that having done something wrong entitles an adult to rehabilitation. It entitles him to punishment. Murder entitles him to execution.

If rehabilitation were our aim, most murderers could be released. Quite often they are "rehabilitated" by the very murder they committed. They are unlikely to commit other crimes. We punish them not for what they may or may not do in the future but for what they have done. . . .

The Romans thought that *"homo homini res sacra"*—every human being should be sacred to every other human being. To enforce the sacredness of human life, the Romans unflinchingly executed murderers.

One may well argue that human life is cheapened when murderers, instead of being executed, are imprisoned as pickpockets are. It is not enough to proclaim human life inviolable. Innocent life is best secured by telling those who would take it that they will forfeit their own life. A society that allows those who took the innocent life of others to live on—albeit in prison for a time—does not protect the lives of its members or hold them sacred. The discontinuity between murder and other crimes should be underlined by the death penalty, not blurred by punishing murderers as one punishes thieves. Murder is not quite so trifling an offense.

To insist that the murderer has the same right to live as his victim pushes egalitarianism too far. It blurs moral distinctions and seems to recognize only physical equalities. His crime morally sets the murderer apart from his victim. The victim did, and therefore the murderer does not, deserve to live. His life cannot be sacred if that of his victim was.

"Capital punishment 'overcompensates' for the violation of justice and moral unity created by serious crimes."

The Death Penalty Is Immoral

Michael E. Endres

Michael E. Endres, Ph.D., is professor of criminal justice at Xavier University in Cincinnati and a member of the Academy of Criminal Justice Sciences. In the following viewpoint, Mr. Endres presents a moral legal argument against the death penalty. He states that capital punishment is immoral because it fails as a valid purpose of punishment.

As you read, consider the following questions:

1. Why, in the opinion of Mr. Endres, is the death penalty not required by any of the general purposes of punishment?
2. What alternatives to the death penalty does the author suggest that would be effective means to deal with dangerous offenders?

These excerpts are reprinted with permission from THE MORALITY OF CAPITAL PUNISHMENT, Equal Justice Under the Law?, copyright 1985 by Michael E. Endres (paper, 160 pages, $5.95) published by Twenty-Third Publications, Mystic, CT 06355.

The first requirement in evaluating the morality of capital punishment is to identify its purposes or objectives. Indeed, whether or not a punishment is initially legal depends upon whether or not it serves a valid goal or purpose of public policy. Obviously, the individual cannot be caused pain or have his rights limited to no good purpose. Likewise, a punishment that inflicts harm on the person can hardly be good or moral if it is purposeless. . . .

Purposes of Punishment

Any form of punishment may be imposed upon the wrongdoer for one or a combination of the following purposes: (1) to protect the community from recidivism by this particular offender (special deterrence), or from criminal offences by others who may profit by the example (general deterrence); (2) to rehabilitate the offender; and (3) to restore the moral order breached by the violation of community norms and the rights of others. As the following discussion shows, capital punishment is not required by any of the general purposes of punishment. Other alternatives may serve better or as well.

Rehabilitation of the Offender. In one case, the death penalty is clearly counterproductive. The second purpose, the rehabilitation of the offender, is obviously inapplicable in the case of capital punishment. The death is no more recuperative in either a social or personal sense than would be the deliberate termination of life in a cancer patient. The American Cancer Society would hardly define the latter form of remission to be a success or cure.

Incapacitation. There is not much question about the death penalty's service in the cause of special deterrence. It is incontestable that the execution of an offender is the most certain way to incapacitate him or eliminate his further offenses against society.

The death penalty is not, of course, the only way to achieve this end. For example, lengthy periods of incarceration may effectively incapacitate the offender when it is necessary to do so. Moreover, other criteria must be considered in judging the fitness of the death penalty. While death may be the most certain prevention, it is also the most extreme. There is some uncertainty in prolonged incarceration or life terms which permit eventual parole; admittedly some statistically small risk of serious reoffending exists. At the same time, there is also a statistically small risk of executing a person who is innocent of serious wrongdoing. There is also a *substantial* risk of executing guilty persons *unjustly*. . . .

Realistic Alternative

There are other, less flawed ways to incapacitate dangerous offenders, if we have the will to use them. For example, life imprisonment without possibility of parole is a realistic alternative for the small number of offenders who are likely to be executed in any given year. And it carries absolutely no risk to the community. Moreover, life imprisonment does not risk irredeemable miscarriages of justice or extenuate inequities that may be created by the malfunctions of the criminal system. . . . It is sufficient to note that there is not indispensability about the final solution.

General Deterrence. The purpose of general deterrence is no doubt the most applicable to capital punishment. If the state may, by taking the life of the grievous offender, deter others from similarly harming the community, the extreme penalty of death might appear to be warranted. In principle, the community's right and obligation to protect the innocent might take priority over the rights of the guilty. Some would still oppose the death penalty on absolute grounds, independent of any purported deterrent effect.

Justice Does Not Demand Death

Perhaps we want retribution on the flesh and bone of a handful of convicted murderers so badly that we're willing to close our eyes to all of the demoralization and danger that come with it. A lot of politicans think so, and they may be right. But if they are, then let's at least look honestly at what we're doing. This lottery of death both comes from and encourages an attitude toward human life that is not reverent, but reckless. . . . Justice does demand that murderers be punished. And common sense demands that society be protected from them. But neither justice nor self-preservation demands that we kill men whom we have already imprisoned.

David Bruck, *The New Republic*, May 20, 1985.

For most opponents of capital punishment, the crux of the problem is, however, deterrence. To say that some punishment is justified by this purpose is not the same as saying that the extreme of capital punishment is justified because it does deter. Another qualification on the dealth penalty as a deterrent has recently been indirectly addressed by the Supreme Court. In ruling that the death penalty was excessive and unconstitutional for the crimes of rape and accomplice to felony murder, the Court recognized the first principle of deterrence: excessive penalties are not acceptable. In analogous terms, a nation has no right to deter other potential aggressors by punishing an enemy in a conventional war with a first strike nuclear attack.

Another implicit aspect of the death penalty as a deterrent is frequently overlooked: there are always alternative pathways to similar ends. The question becomes then, what is the most effective deterrent among alternative punishments? In other words, what must really be determined about the death penalty is whether or not it is *marginally* deterrent. To what extent does the death penalty prevent targeted crimes more effectively than alternatives such as life imprisonment? Opponents of capital punishment would generally be unwilling to concede that capital punishment has social utility if it is not established that it is a superior deterrent. . . .

Restore the Order of Justice

Perhaps the most complicated of all the purposes of punishment is that of restoring the moral order and the order of justice. There are two related, but qualitatively distinct interpretations that could be given to this purpose. On one side, there are motives inspired by the emotional elements in human nature. There is the primordial urge to lash back at an offender, the natural tendency to return pain for pain received. Such reactions are basic to clan justice, for example, the *les talionis* of the Old Testament. Collective punishments, including the capital kind, are frequently rationalized on such grounds. It is often argued that when the community is unwilling or unable to control crime through the imposition of stringent penalties, the individual is encouraged to take the law into his own hands. In fiction, personal avengers and vigilantes are depicted as deriving deep-seated emotional satisfaction in meting out just deserts to malefactors. Readers or audiences respond with similar feelings. No doubt the sometime popularity of capital puishment in American public opinion reflects the ebb and flow of emotional needs.

Opponents of capital punishment tend to dismiss such retributive motives out of hand, to condemn them as primitive and animalistic. On the other hand, there are compelling considerations of justice which ought not to be lightly dismissed. If justice is essentially fairness, we are required to ask, is it fair that one profits from another's loss? Should we not feel it grossly unfair when innocent life is taken to gratify the needs of the slayer for economic gain, power, vengeance, or whatever? Quite aside from the need to protect society, doesn't the offender *owe* something to those who survive the victim—to family, to friends, to the community as a whole? Thus, in whatever form, punishment may also be seen as compensatory. In the civil law of torts, judgments are rendered and penalties imposed on one individual or party in behalf of another individual or party. Under the criminal law, the obligation of the offender is to the community as a whole, aside from any additional responsibilities which may be imposed on behalf of the victims or their kin.

Reinforce Social Unity

There is a related matter of no small importance. Society is a moral unity. It is a system of social interactions which binds us to one another. An offense by one harms the well-being of all. Life in human society would be impossible if we could not have

65

reasonable expectations of one another. While we can never afford to be naive and must always be wary of others, particularly when we do not know them, neither can we live together without a fundamental level of trust. The butcher, the baker, the druggist must be able to exchange their commodities without fear of adulteration or tainting by uncleanliness or poison. No matter how defensively he drives, the motorist must believe that people will not drive cars when they have had too much to drink, or that people will obey traffic signals. The alternatives to mutual trust and mutual expectations are alienation and paralysis. Life in human society would be impossible if one could violate the law with impunity. In part, the criminal law exists to reaffirm our need and our ability to depend on one another. Collective sanctions exist, therefore, not only to incapacitate or deter or rehabilitate the offender. They also exist to restore a moral unity uninterrupted by violations of trust and to be sure the offender atones for his wrongdoing. Indeed, without this dynamic, the rehabilitative purpose of punishment would lose its meaning. Individual reform is the flip side of the requirement to compensate others in some way for that which has been taken from them.

'BAD'   'GOOD'

© Miller/Rothco

Note that semantic arguments about what constitutes punishment are avoided here. . . . What is of concern now is the legitimacy of punishment in the interests of justice and the moral solidarity which binds us to one another. Such interests ought to be assigned to the more primitive level and dismissed as simply vengeful.

66

Vengeful motives for the death penalty ought to be repudiated. They emanate from the dark side of man, which is human, but not preeminent or noble. Critics of capital punishment are quite correct in identifying its spirit and practice with those cultural dark ages in which people resolved their differences by violent force, in which superior force meant right, and in which human and animal violence was popular public entertainment. . . .

Capital Punishment Is Excessive

[If punishment is justifiable as a means of restoring justice and the moral order, it does not necessarily follow that capital punishment is just. First of all, there is the question of how well capital punishment may serve to restore justice and moral unity. Beyond that issue, there are other criteria to consider. The death penalty is not absolutely demanded by justice and social unity, even in grave crimes; some opponents would consider it excessive for these purposes.]Neither justice nor unity is a simple matter of an eye-for-an-eye or a tooth-for-a-tooth; a principle of justice that grew out of vengeful motivations. The history of Western jurisprudence shows a steady progression away from tit for tat in punishment, especially in its corporal forms. We no longer tolerate the draconian barbarity of extorted confessions or punish criminals by maiming the offending physical organ.[Punishments that arise out of a thirst for vengeance are inhumane, counterproductive, and unnecessary. Other stringent measures might serve as well to restore the order of justice and moral unity. Some proponents of capital punishment inconsistently argue that prolonged incarceration under life sentences is actually more punitive than the death penalty. A Gary Gilmore may prefer execution, a Charlie Brooks, Jr., may fight to the bitter end to live, even within grim prison walls. There are alternatives severe enough to be proportional, even to grave crimes. Life imprisonment or prolonged periods of incarceration, for 25 to 30 years, are indeed severe penalties.]

[Then, at worst, capital punishment "overcompensates" for the violation of justice and moral unity created by serious crimes. Under those circumstances, it is an unacceptable way to right the balance. . . . In sum, . . . the death penalty serves no rehabilitative purpose; it exceeds the requirements of justice and social unity; alternatives to it may serve the same purpose as well; finally, the incapacitation or special deterrence of a given offender is insured by execution, but there are other effective ways to inhibit reoffending.]

"Capital punishment . . . serves to remind us of the majesty of the moral order that is embodied in our law, and of the terrible consequences of its breach."

The Death Penalty Dignifies Society

Walter Berns

Walter Berns is John M. Olin Distinguished Scholar at the American Enterprise Institute. A noted educator and writer, he is the author of the landmark book on the death penalty, *For Capital Punishment: Crime and the Morality of the Death Penalty.* In the following viewpoint, Mr. Berns argues that anger morally justifies the execution of society's worst criminals to uphold the dignity of law and order.

As you read, consider the following questions:

1. What, according to the author, is the principle of punishing criminals?
2. Why does the author believe that there is a moral connection between anger and human dignity?
3. According to the author, why does criminal law need to be made "awful"?

From FOR CAPITAL PUNISHMENT by Walter Berns. Copyright © 1979 by Walter Berns. Reprinted by permission of Basic Books, Inc., Publishers.

Until recently, my business did not require me to think about the punishment of criminals in general or the legitimacy and efficacy of capital punishment in particular. In a vague way, I was aware of the disagreement among professionals concerning the purpose of punishment—whether it was intended to deter others, to rehabilitate the criminal, or to pay him back—but like most laymen I had no particular reason to decide which purpose was right or to what extent they may all have been right. I did know that retribution was held in ill repute among criminologists and jurists—to them, retribution was a fancy name for revenge, and revenge was barbaric—and, of course, I knew that capital punishment had the support only of policemen, prison guards and some local politicians. . . . The intellectual community denounced it as both unnecessary and immoral. It was the phenomenon of Simon Wiesenthal that allowed me to understand why the intellectuals were wrong and why the police, the politicians, and the majority of the voters were right: We punish criminals principally in order to pay them back, and we execute the worst of them out of moral necessity. . . .

Be Angry with Criminals

Why should anyone devote his life—more than thirty years of it!—exclusively to the task of hunting down the Nazi war criminals who survived World War II and escaped punishment? Wiesenthal says his conscience forces him "to bring the guilty ones to trial." But why punish them? . . . We surely don't expect to rehabilitate them, and it would be foolish to think that by punishing them we might thereby deter others. The answer, I think, is clear: We want to punish them in order *to pay them back*. We think they must be made to pay for their crimes with their lives, and we think that we, the survivors of the world they violated, may legitimately exact that payment because we, too, are their victims. By punishing them, we demonstrate that there are laws that bind men across generations as well as across (and within) nations, that we are not simply isolated individuals, each pursuing his selfish interests and connected with others by a mere contract to live and let live. To state it simply, Wiesenthal allows us to see that it is right, morally right, to be angry with criminals and to express that anger publicly, officially, and in an appropriate manner, which may require the worst of them to be executed.

Modern civil-libertarian opponents of capital punishment do not understand this. They say that to execute a criminal is to deny his human dignity; they also say that the death penalty is not useful, that nothing useful is accomplished by executing anyone. Being utilitarians, they are essentially selfish men, distrustful of passion, who do not understand the connection between anger and justice, and between anger and human dignity.

Anger is expressed or manifested on those occasions when someone has acted in a manner that is thought to be unjust, and one of its origins is the opinion that men are responsible, and should be held responsible, for what they do. . . . And in holding particular men responsible, it pays them the respect that is due them as men. Anger recognizes that only men have the capacity to be moral beings and, in so doing, acknowledges the dignity of human beings. Anger is somehow connected with justice, and it is this that modern penology has not understood; it tends, on the whole, to regard anger as a selfish indulgence.

Murder Deserves Death

When I think of the thousands of inhabitants of Death Rows in the hundreds of prisons in this country, I don't react the way the kindly souls do—with revulsion that the state would take these human lives.

My reaction is: What's taking us so long? Let's get that electrical current flowing. Drop those pellets now!

Whenever I argue this with friends who have opposite views, they say that I don't have enough regard for that most marvelous of miracles—human life.

Just the opposite: It's because I have so much regard for human life that I favor capital punishment. Murder is the most terrible crime there is. Anything less than the death penalty is an insult to the victim and society. It says, in effect, that we don't value the victim's life enough to punish the killer fully.

Mike Royko, *Chicago Sun-Times*, September 1983.

Anger can, of course, be that; and if someone does not become angry with an insult or an injury suffered unjustly, we tend to think he does not think much of himself. But it need not be selfish, not in the sense of being provoked only by an injury suffered by oneself. There were many angry men in America when President Kennedy was killed; one of them—Jack Ruby—took it upon himself to exact the punishment that, if indeed deserved, ought to have been exacted by the law. There were perhaps even angrier men when Martin Luther King, Jr., was killed, for King, more than anyone else at the time, embodied a people's quest for justice; the anger—more, the "black rage"—expressed on that occasion was simply a manifestation of the great change that had occurred among black men in America, a change wrought in large part by King and his associates in the civil-rights movement: the servility and fear of the past had been replaced by pride and anger, and the treatment that had formerly been accepted as a matter of course or as if it were deserved was now seen for what it was, unjust and unacceptable. King preached love, but the movement he led depended on anger as well as love, and that anger was not despicable, being neither selfish nor unjustified. On the contrary, it was a reflection of what was called solidarity and may more accurately be called a profound caring for others, black for other blacks, white for blacks, and, in the world King was trying to build, American for other Americans. If men are not saddened when someone else suffers, or angry when someone else suffers unjustly, the implication is that they do not care for anyone other than themselves or that they lack some quality that befits a man. When we criticize them for this, we acknowledge that they ought to care for others. If men are not angry when a neighbor suffers at the hands of a criminal, the implication is that their moral faculties have been corrupted, that they are not good citizens.

Criminals Are Objects of Anger

Criminals are properly the objects of anger, and the perpetrators of terrible crimes—for example, Lee Harvey Oswald and James Earl Ray—are properly the objects of great anger. They have done more than inflict an injury on an isolated individual; they have violated the foundations of trust and friendship, the necessary elements of a moral community, the only community worth living in. A moral community, unlike a hive of bees or a hill of ants, is one whose members are expected freely to obey the laws and, unlike those in a tyranny, are trusted to obey the laws. The criminal has violated that trust, and in so doing has injured not merely his immediate victim but the community as such. He has called into question the very possibility of that community by suggesting that men cannot be trusted to respect freely the property, the person, and the dignity of those with whom they are associated. If, then, men are not angry when someone else is robbed, raped, or murdered, the implication is that no moral community exists, because those men do not care for anyone other then themselves. Anger is an expression of that caring, and society needs men who care for one another, who share their pleasures and their pains, and do so for the sake of the others. It is the passion that can cause us to act for reasons having nothing to do with selfish or mean calculation; indeed, when educated, it can become a generous passion, the passion that protects the community or country by demanding punishment for its enemies. It is the stuff from which heroes are made. . . .

Criminal Law Must Be Awful

Capital punishment . . . serves to remind us of the majesty of the moral order that is embodied in our law, and of the terrible consequences of its breach. The law must not be understood to be merely a statute that we enact or repeal at our will, and obey or disobey at our convenience—especially not the criminal law. Wherever law is regarded as merely statutory, men will soon enough disobey it, and will learn how to do so without any inconvenience to themselves. The criminal law must possess a dignity far beyond that possessed by mere statutory enactment or utilitarian and self-interested calculations. The most powerful means we have to give it that dignity is to authorize it to impose the ultimate penalty. The criminal law must be made awful, by which I mean inspiring, or commanding "profound respect or reverential fear." It must remind us of the moral order by which alone we can live as *human* beings, and in America, now that the Supreme Court has outlawed banishment, the only punishment that can do this is capital punishment.

"State-sanctioned executions expose more of the violence and injustice that are in us all. It is a dehumanizing ritual."

The Death Penalty Degrades Society

John Cole Vodicka

John Cole Vodicka works for the Office for Prisoner and Community Justice, Oakland Catholic Charities. He has long been involved in work against the death penalty in both California and Louisiana. In the following viewpoint, Mr. Vodicka illustrates why he believes the imposition of the death penalty harms society and creates more victims.

As you read, consider the following questions:

1. How, according to Mr. Vodicka, does the imposition of the death penalty become a degrading act?
2. In the opinion of the author, what is the brutalizing effect of the ritual of capital punishment?
3. Why does the author believe that legitimate retaliation sows the seeds of violence?

John Cole Vodicka, "All-Embracing Affect of the Death Penalty," *The California Prisoner,* January 1985. Reprinted with permission.

[No matter how one feels about the death penalty, no matter what arguments one uses to bolster his or her position, one thing seems absolutely certain to me: State-sanctioned executions expose more of the violence and injustice that are in us all. It is a dehumanizing ritual, one that brings more injury to each of us.]

[I have been a lifelong opponent of the death penalty. My opposition stems from a variety of reasons: Capital punishment does not deter; it is applied arbitrarily and in a discriminatory fashion; it is cruel and unusual punishment; it is irreversible; and it mocks the commandment, "Thou shalt not kill."]

I also oppose the death penalty because in my work I have come to know the issue in human terms, in the names and faces of those involved or caught up in this grisly business. Some of these faces are of prisoners who have been executed; in the last 12 months I have lost six friends to the electric chair. Other faces are of the condemned prisoners' families, the families of their victims, of prison officials and guards, of chaplains, lawyers, judges, elected officials and witnesses to executions. And there are the angry faces of those who, out of frustration and fear, have told me they believe the death penalty, whether it "works" or not, is "just desert" for anyone convicted of murder. Countless faces and names, each in his or her own way, a victim of a degrading process that prohibits us from recognizing each other's humanity.

More Victims

On May 25, 1979, I stood with several hundred people in front of the Starke, Florida penitentiary, where John Spenkelink was about to be executed. We were there to pray and to stand in opposition to the impending execution. Standing nearby, though, were several dozen people, a coffin perched atop their Winnebago, chanting "Go, Sparky, Go!" Some were wearing T-shirts that depicted an electric chair with the words, "1 down, 131 to go!"

On December 7, 1982, hundreds of college students gathered and gawked outside the Texas Penitentiary at Huntsville and celebrated the impending lethal-injection execution of Charlie Brooks, Jr. They ate popcorn and drank beer, taunting those of us gathered there standing in silent opposition. Some of the students held up handmade signs that read, "Kill Him in Vein" and "Put the Animal to Sleep."

On October 12, 1984, across the street from the Virginia Prison in Richmond, rowdy, beer-drinking death-penalty proponents gathered to cheer on the execution of Linwood Briley. They too displayed signs that conveyed a lynchmob mentality. "Fry, nigger, fry!" read one poster. "Burn Briley, Burn," encouraged another. The demonstrators set off firecrackers when word finally came from the prison that Briley was dead.

74

And here in California earlier this year condemned prisoner Robert Harris lost another round of appeals, thereby temporarily clearing the way for his execution date to be set. The next day, I am told, the switchboard at San Quentin lit up, as dozens of people, including a Los Angeles County district attorney, phoned the warden's office requesting to be an offical "witness" to the gassing of Robert Harris.

One of the callers was Steven Baker, the father of the child Robert Harris is accused of killing. Baker believes the death penalty will ease his pain, ease his anger. But listen: "Every time Harris files an appeal and his name gets in the papers, myself and

"Let's move it along! . . . we've got 1,268 to go!"

the families have to go through it all over again," Baker says. "The longer this has dragged on the more my rage has been directed at the criminal justice system."

Revenge and Retaliation

[It is clear to me that the ritual of capital punishment brutalizes us all; it extends the violence, provokes anger, and hinders, rather than encourages, healing. The death penalty exposes a system which is based on revenge and retaliation. To the detriment of us all, it justifies lethal vengeance]

Virginia Governor Charles Robb, when asked about the pro-death penalty demonstration in Richmond on the night Linwood Briley was executed, called it "inappropriate behavior." But my colleague and friend Marie Deans, who worked to halt Briley's electrocution and who is herself a family member of a murder victim, remarked that the crowd's behavior was "no different than Governor Robb's allowing Briley to be executed, no more inappropriate than what occurred behind those prison walls."

"The ultimate result of this and every execution," Deans said, "is nothing less than a total disregard for life."

I am convinced that as we deny a death row prisoner his or her humanity, so do we lose a little more of our own.

Several years ago my friend Tim Baldwin faced imminent execution in Louisiana. Then, at the last hour, we were successful in obtaining a stay order from a panel of federal judges. A frustrated, vengeful public expressed its outrage. "Killer Cheats Chair" screamed one daily newspaper headline. And on one popular New Orleans radio talk show, the host suggested that not only should Baldwin have been electrocuted but that I should have been forced to sit in Baldwin's lap! (Tim Baldwin is one of those faces; he was ultimately executed on September 10, 1984.)

Circle of Tragedy

[The death penalty doesn't end the suffering, it prolongs it. It doesn't limit the tragedy, it widens it. It doesn't abate the anger, it keeps the wounds open. Each execution draws dozens and dozens more people into its web. The circle of tragedy is always expanding and ultimately, all of us are affected.]

During the periods of publicity and ritual surrounding executions in several Southern states, I have watched with sadness as victims' families and friends often become public spectacles. They are subjected to infrequent indignities and damaging publicity at the time of trial. Healing is retarded as they are dragged through the experience again, usually years later, at the time of appeal and execution. "For many," says Howard Zehr, director of the Mennonite Central Committee's Office of Criminal Justice, "the ritual of the death penalty takes precedence over the ritual of mourning and remembrance."

I know of at least one Southern prison warden who, when asked how an execution affected him personally, tearfully explained: "This society makes me do its dirty work. I have to take care of these prisoners—one year, two years, maybe even 10 years. And then I have to kill them."

[The death penalty creates more victims.]

Death Penalty Is Bad Company

[Sometimes you can judge the morality of a practice by the company it keeps: Executions hang out in the world's seediest neighborhoods. Indeed, contrasting those nations still engaged in capital punishment with those that abstain is a course in moral geography we cannot ignore.

The Angolite, November/December, 1983.]

Former San Quentin warden Lawrence Wilson, who participated in a number of executions, told Oakland freelance journalist Michael Kroll: "You never get used to seeing [an execution]. You get sort of a sinking, sick feeling. After all, there's a guy in front of you, and he struggles to stay alive, but his life support system fails him. He expires before your eyes."

[The death penalty dehumanizes.]

When Robert Wayne Williams was executed in Louisiana last December, Governor David Treen, who refused to grant clemency to Williams, broke down and cried. He called his decision not to spare Williams' life "the most agonizing I've ever had to face." Sam Dalton, Williams' attorney, said, "I felt like I had been amputated when I heard he had been executed. It was a loss that I just couldn't believe."

The circle of tragedy grows.

And Howard Brodie, an artist for CBS News who witnessed the 1967 execution of Aaron Mitchell in California and the 1979 execution of John Spenkelink in Florida, called those experiences "the most dehumanizing of my entire life."

Extending the Pain

["The death penalty only allows us to extend the pain," says Virginia activist Marie Deans. "It allows us to continue to blame one another, to turn against one another, to learn to hate better."]

[Yes, I have seen the full effects of capital punishment. It is measurable in the strain and stress of broken families, ill health, alcoholism, mental breakdown, hospitalization, and for those who survive these ills, in a brutalization born of desperation. It is a brutalization that mars not only the lives of prisoners but of all those touched by the death penalty.]

[Colin Turnbull, the noted anthropologist, has undertaken a study of the death penalty and its effect on society. And he concludes:

"Until we face the harsh facts of what happens on death row and in the execution room, in the witness room and in the offices and homes of the prison officials, lawyers and judges, we are not entitled to have an opinion on capital punishment and call it just. If we were really concerned with the well-being of society, there would be little or no need for the death penalty in the first place."

There's the rub. Are we really concerned with society's welfare or are we content in merely providing ourselves with the illusion that something is being done? Do we really believe we will be able to get rid of evil by defining it out of the human species? Or is it no more than revenge, the need to strike back, to get even?

No Right to Get Even

"If it is vengeance, that's bad for society," says New York Governor Mario Cuomo, one of four current U.S. governors opposed to the death penalty. "We don't have the right to get even. It reduces the value of life, and we've done that enough in past years."

But will we ever learn? Will we ever admit to our past mistakes and begin to explore more constructive alternatives to the death penalty, alternatives that still convey firmly and clearly that murder is wrong? I hope so.

I know it is not easy for any of us to ward off bitterness and the desire for retaliation. But I also believe that for too long we have treated violence with violence and that's why it never seems to end.

Coretta Scott King has lost both a husband and mother-in-law to murder. Still, she speaks out powerfully against the death penalty, against killing people who kill people. Hers, too, is a face I cannot forget. Nor can I forget her words:

"The truth is, we all pay for the death penalty because every time the state kills somebody, our society loses its humanity and compassion and we sow the seeds of violence. We legitimize retaliation as the way to deal with conflict. Yes, we all pay. And in this sense the death penalty means cruel and unusual punishment for not only the condemned prisoner but for the innocent as well, for all of us."

"There is no inconsistency between moral disapproval of unnecessarily killing the innocent and the judicial execution of the guilty."

Religious Views Support the Death Penalty

Haven Bradford Gow

Haven Bradford Gow is a Wilbur Foundation Literary Fellow in Arlington Heights, Illinois. In the following viewpoint, Mr. Gow contends that the death penalty is moral on both religious and humanitarian principles and that religious teachings prove that the death penalty upholds the dignity of human life as ordered by scripture.

As you read, consider the following questions:

1. What evidence does the author give showing that the Roman Catholic Church teaches that the death penalty is legitimate and necessary?
2. How does the author use Protestant teaching to support his belief that capital punishment upholds God's law for order in society?
3. Why does Mr. Gow believe that the death penalty deters crimes like murder?

Haven Bradford Gow, "Should Religious Support Capital Punishment?" *Human Events*, March 2, 1985. Reprinted with permission.

Recent executions in North Carolina, Mississippi, Texas, Louisiana and Florida have focused attention on the morality or immorality of capital punishment.

In North Carolina, 52-year-old Margie Velma Barfield recently was executed by lethal injection for the 1978 murder of her lover. Mrs. Barfield, who was the first woman executed in this country in 22 years, was sentenced to death for putting ant poison in the beer and tea of her fiance. She also confessed to poisoning her mother and two elderly people for whom she worked as a live-in housekeeper.

In Mississippi, a man was executed in a gas chamber for raping, sodomizing and murdering a young girl, while a man in Texas received the death penalty for poisoning to death his son.

On April 5, 1984, two murderers—one in Florida, the other in Louisiana—were executed on the same day. The Louisiana man was executed for murdering a teenage boy and raping and murdering the boy's female companion, while the Florida man was executed for the sex slaying of a young boy.

Some religious people opposed to capital punishment insist that the death penalty is "cruel and unusual punishment," and that it is contrary to moral and religious principles. They argue that, instead of executing murderers, society should opt for "prisoner rehabilitation" or lifetime sentences with no possibility of parole.

Conference of Bishops

The National Conference of Catholic Bishops of the United States, for example, has come out against the death penalty, maintaining that it is "uncivilized," "barbaric" and "inhumane"; the organization contends that capital punishment is an assault on the sanctity of human life and, moreover, has linked its opposition to the death penalty with its opposition to abortion.

Even so, many Catholic lay persons and theologians persist in their view that it is *not* a contradiction for religious people to oppose abortion-on-demand and, at the same time, favor capital punishment for, say, someone who has raped and murdered a child. They reason that the unborn child is innocent of wrongdoing, while the rapist-murderer has taken the life of another human being.

Sixty-eight-year-old Rocco Cordaro, a staff member of the Nicholas Lattof YMCA in Des Plaines, Ill., is the faithful husband of Madeline Cordaro and the father of three sons and one daughter. He also is a devout Catholic who sharply dissents from the controversial stand taken on the death penalty by the National Conference of Catholic Bishops of the United States.

In the view of dedicated Catholic Rocco Cordaro, the bishops' stand on the death penalty demonstrates a misguided "concern for the criminals instead of for the victims of crime and their families. The innocent people—men, women, and children—who are murdered weren't given any chance, so why should we feel sorry for sadistic murderers like Speck and Gacy? Why should we feel more sympathy for the killers instead of for the families of the victims?''

Punish Sadistic Murderers

Sadistic murderers such as Gacy, Speck, Bundy, Bittaker and Heirens, says Cordaro, ''can't be rehabilitated. How many criminals have been let out of prison only to go on killing, raping and stealing? Why should we allow criminals to harm innocent children, and get away with what they do?''

Cordaro was asked about the argument that the Commandment ''Thou shalt not kill'' means that society does not have the moral right to execute convicted murderers. He responds: ''The Commandment also has to apply to the murderer. What about justice being done to the murderers who didn't respect the Commandment in the first place?''

He adds: ''We can't have our jails filled with people who rape and murder. Everyone's life is sacred—why, then, does the criminal feel he has the right or authority to kill? The lives of the victims also are sacred.''

Some Christian scholars and theologians—Catholic and Protestant—readily agree that capital punishment is a morally acceptable way to punish sadistic murderers.

The Sixth Commandment

The Bible is our greatest source of moral inspiration. Opponents of the death penalty frequently cite the sixth of the Ten Commandments [''Thou shalt not kill''] in an attempt to prove that capital punishment is divinely proscribed. In the original Hebrew, however, the Sixth Commandment reads, ''Thou Shalt Not Commit Murder,'' and the Torah specifies capital punishment for a variety of offenses. The biblical viewpoint has been upheld by philosophers throughout history.

Edward I. Koch, *The New Republic*, April 15, 1985.

For example, Father Richard Roach, S.J., a Marquette University scholar, argues that it is *not* a contradiction for religious people to oppose abortion and, at the same time, support capital punishment. As he explains, ''Abortion is absolutely prohibited. It is always evil. No one can ever abort a 'guilty' baby, so the act can never be right. This is not the case, however, with either capital punishment or killing in a just or defensive war.''

Father Roach observes that, in cases of capital punishment and killing in a just war, ''the deadly deed can be the right thing to

81

do. It is only murder, along with its subdivisions suicide and abortion, which God's law absolutely prohibits. (Murder is the direct or intentional killing of the innocent.)

"Therefore, we should be inconsistent if we classified an act which God's law absolutely prohibits—namely, abortion—along with acts which God's law does not absolutely prohibit, namely, capital punishment and the conduct of just war."

Father Roach declares: "The upshot of all this is that trying to put abortion, capital punishment and war in one package makes chaos of Catholic morals and can lead one to misinterpret God's law so that, at least by omission, he will do what is objectively evil; namely, refuse to defend the innocent."

Catholic scholar Father James Reilly, M.S., also supports capital punishment, pointing out that the official teaching of the Roman Catholic church favors the death penalty. Concerning the argument that capital punishment is a morally unjustifiable attack on the sanctity of human life, Father Reilly responds: "I consider it my duty as a Catholic priest and as a citizen to point out that that statement goes directly counter to the official teaching of the Roman Catholic Church on the subject of capital punishment."

Father Reilly points out that "the Roman Catechism of the Council of Trent, promulgated in 1566 by Pope (and Saint) Pius V" makes clear that the death penalty is a morally acceptable way to punish murderers:

The Fifth Commandment

"I quote from the Chapter on the Fifth Commandment of God (with regard to the specific question: May the State put criminals to death?): 'Another kind of slaying belongs to the civil authorities, to whom is entrusted the power of life and death, by the legal and judicious exercise of which they punish the guilty and protect the innocent. The just use of this power, far from involving the crime of murder, is an act of paramount obedience to this Commandment which prohibits murder. The end (or purpose) of the Commandment is the preservation and security of human life. Now the punishment inflicted by the civil authority [evidently meaning the actual execution of criminals], which is the legitimate avenger of crimes, naturally tend to this end, since they give security to life by repressing outrage and violence.' "

Father Reilly also notes that "From the time of St. Paul (*Romans 13:4*) until today this has always been the official teaching of the Catholic Church and only the Holy See or a General Council has the authority to change it. The curious thing is that those Catholics who have repeatedly condemned capital punishment and have often, apparently at least, declared it immoral, *never* refer to that passage from the Roman Catechism. It may be that they are unaware of it, but such ignorance is, in my opinion, inexcusable."

According to Father Pierre Lachance, O.P., of St. Anne Parish in Fall River, Mass., "Thomas Aquinas reflects the common and traditional teaching of the Church, allowing capital punishment for serious crimes, when the crime is proved and when the common good requires it."

Capital Punishment Is Liturgical

"Most human beings feel restless if there is no moral order," says Catholic theologian Michael Novak. "They feel discontent. Their spirit feels dissatisfied. Something is 'not right.'"

"Capital punishment is a liturgical act. Its purpose is to reassert the moral order of the community."

Bob Hutchinson, *Salt*, June 1984.

For St. Thomas, "Every part is directed to the whole, as imperfect to perfect; wherefore, every part is naturally for the sake of the whole. For this reason we observe that if the health of the whole body demands the excision of a member, through its being decayed or infectious to the other members, it will be both praiseworthy and advantageous to the whole community to have it cut away.

"Now every individual person is compared to the whole community, as part to whole. Therefore, if a man be dangerous and infectious to the community on account of some sin [crime], it is praiseworthy and advantageous that he be killed in order to safeguard the common good, since 'little leaven corrupts the whole lump!' (*I Corinthians 5:6*)."

Supported by Catholic Teaching

Traditional Catholic teaching maintains that capital punishment is morally justified and a much-needed deterrent to criminals. As Father Lachance points out, "The traditional thinking of theologians is that capital punishment is the most effective deterrent to crime. . . . One thing for sure, society must be protected against murderers, against those who pose a serious threat to society."

True, "Incarceration and rehabilitation would certainly be a better solution if it were feasible. But we all know the extremely low rate of rehabilitation in our society."

Father Lachance moreover observes that "Society must be protected against criminals. That is legitimate, so that capital punishment becomes legitimate and necessary if that is the only effective way to safeguard the common good. This means that the individual who poses a threat to the life of others loses his own right to live."

Father Lachance adds: "There is no question but that capital punishment was not only allowed but mandated in the Old Testament. In the New Law, Paul recognizes the legitimacy of capital punishment, writing to the Romans: 'It is not without purpose that the ruler carries the sword. He is God's servant, to inflict his avenging wrath upon the wrongdoer (*Romans 13:4*).'"

No Inconsistency

For example, concerning the argument that, if one is to be consistent, one must oppose *both* abortion and capital punishment, Princeton University scholar Paul Ramsey responds that "abortion and capital punishment are two *different* questions. There is no inconsistency between moral disapproval of unnecessarily killing the innocent and the judicial execution of the guilty."

According to the Protestant scholar and journalist Rev. G. Aiken Taylor, "most Christians tend to confuse the Christian personal ethic with the requirements of social order. In other words, we tend to apply what the Bible teaches us about how we—personally—should behave toward our neighbors with what the Bible teaches about how to preserve order in society."

Rev. Aiken affirms that "Capital punishment is specifically enjoined in the Bible. 'Who sheddeth man's blood, by man shall his blood be shed' (*Genesis 9:6*). This command is fully agreeable to the Sixth Commandment, 'Thou shalt not kill,'(*Exodus 20:13*), because the two appear in the same context. Exactly 25 verses after saying 'Thou shalt not kill,' the Law says, 'He that smiteth a man so that he may die, shall be surely put to death' (*Exodus 21:12*)."

Moreover, the *Exodus* reference is not the only one which supports capital punishment. For example, *Leviticus 24:17* says: "He who kills a man shall be put to death." *Numbers 35:30-31* declares: "If anyone kills a person, the murderer shall be put to death on the evidence of witnesses. . . . Moreover, you shall accept no ransom for the life of a murderer who is guilty of death; but he shall be put to death. . . ."

Capital Punishment Must Stand

According to educator Jacob Vellenga, "No one can deny that the execution of a murderer is a horrible spectacle. But we must not forget that murder is more horrible. The penalty should be exacted only after the guilt is established beyond the shadow of a doubt and only for wanton, willful, premeditated murder. But the law of capital punishment must stand, no matter how often a jury recommends mercy." He adds that "The law of capital punishment must stand as a silent but powerful witness to the sacredness of God-given life. Words are not enough to show that life is sacred. Active justice must be administered when the sacredness of life is violated."

In the measured judgment of Protestant clergyman and scholar Rev. Reuben Hahn of Mt. Prospect, Ill., "God himself instituted the death penalty (*Genesis 9:6*) and Christ regarded capital punishment as a just penalty for murder (*Matthew 26:52*). God gave to government the legitimate authority to use capital punishment to restrain murder and punish murderers. Not to inflict the death penalty is a flagrant disregard for God's divine law which recognizes the dignity of human life as a product of God's creation. Life is sacred, and that is why God instituted the death penalty—as a way to protect innocent human life."

Rev. Hahn adds: "The Commandment 'Thou shalt not kill' was given to everybody—including murderers. Consequently, whoever takes innocent human life forfeits his own right to live."

Death Penalty Is Just

To be sure, despite these formidable moral and religious arguments for the death penalty, some religious people—lay persons, scholars and theologians—will continue to maintain that capital punishment is "cruel and unusual punishment" and contrary to religious or humanitarian principles. In my view, however, the death penalty is justified for two reasons:

First, the death penalty helps deter crimes like murder. As the late FBI Director J. Edgar Hoover observed, "The professional law enforcement officer is convinced from experience that the hardened criminal has been and is deterred from killing based on the prospect of the death penalty."

A study conducted by the Los Angeles Police Department in 1970 and 1971 buttresses Hoover's observation. Ninety-nine criminals participated in the study, each giving his reason why he committed his crime unarmed or did not use a weapon. The study revealed a 5-to-1 ratio of deterrence over non-deterrence as reported by people in the best position to make such a judgment: The criminals themselves.

Second, the death penalty is justified on moral grounds. When, for example, someone has raped and murdered a child, that person has relinquished his right to live. Capital punishment in such a case is an act of restitution and demonstrates that a society and legal system are genuinely dedicated to preserving and protecting the rights and safety of the people. Charity also must be displayed towards the victims of crimes and their families.

If society has the moral right and obligation to act in collective self-defense against aggression emanating from *without* (for example, against Nazi and communist assaults on freedom and human rights), then society likewise has the moral right and obligation to defend itself against aggression emanating from *within* (for example, against people who rape and murder children).

*"In our theological deliberations we have come to
the conclusion that the imposition of the death
penalty is inconsistent with our efforts to
promote respect for human life."*

Religious Views Denounce
the Death Penalty

Religious Leaders in Florida

Florida's eight Roman Catholic bishops and eighteen other leaders
of Christian communities released their statement on capital
punishment at five simultaneous news conferences across the state
on November 26, 1984. In the following viewpoint, the authors
of the letter conclude that capital punishment contradicts the
teachings of love and mercy in scripture and is harmful to society.

As you read, consider the following questions:

1. What do the authors mean when they say that the value of
   human life is grounded in the sovereignty of God?
2. In what ways is justice served by a sentence of life imprisonment, according to the authors?
3. In the opinion of the authors, why is the death penalty a
   moral trap that extends human violence?

Origins, "The Moral Consequences of Capital Punishment," December 27, 1984.

This letter is intended to shed light, to stimulate discussion and to encourage moral discourse among Christians. It is limited to a single topic: the increasing use of capital punishment as an instrument of public policy. . . .

We hold that capital punishment is not necessary to any legitimate goal of the state and that its use threatens to undermine belief in the inherent worth of human life and the inalienable dignity of the human estate. Our belief in the value of human life stems from the worship we offer to the Creator of human life and from the teaching of Scripture that each human is created in the image of God.

We affirm that the value of human life is not contingent on the moral rectitude of human beings or human institutions. It is grounded in the sovereignty of God, who alone vests his creatures with the dignity of personhood. In our theological deliberations we have come to the conclusion that the imposition of the death penalty is inconsistent with our efforts to promote respect for human life, to stem the tide of violence in our society and to embody the message of God's redemptive love. In times when life is cheapened and threatened on all fronts, the value and uniqueness of every human life merits profound respect, strong reaffirmation and vigorous proclamation.

Climate of Violence

In time, the use of capital punishment will harden and debase our life together. It institutionalizes revenge and retribution, which are the enemies of peace. It gives official sanction to a climate of violence. It is precisely because of such longer-range concerns—especially our passionate concern for the brutalization and victimization of children and women and men—that we raise the question whether the death penalty makes citizens safer.

Research suggests that the death penalty aggravates the level of violence in society instead of diminishing it. The abolition of capital punishment, which we favor, would nurture the public hope that the cycle of violence can be broken.

It is, after all, a part of our ministry to comfort those whose injury or whose bereavement is the result of violent crime. It is in the midst of such tragic circumstances that we become aware of the moral trap in which we find ourselves: that a commitment to wrathful retribution compounds and extends the horror of human violence rather than subduing it.

Scripture and Capital Punishment

The Old Testament prescribes the death penalty for a wide variety of offenses. Many of them have been committed by respected members of the citizenry: adultery (Lv. 20:10; Dt. 22:22ff), idolatry (Ex. 20:3-5; Dt. 13:1-10, 17:2-7), false prophecy in the name of God (Dt. 18:20-22), laboring on the sabbath (Ex. 31:14-15, 35:2), strik-

87

ing or cursing or rebelling against a parent (Ex. 20:12ff, 21:17, Lv. 19:3, 20:9; Dt. 21:18ff), prostitution or harlotry under certain circumstances (Lv. 21:9, Dt. 22:20-21), sorcery (Ex. 22:18; Lv. 20:27), cursing God (Ex. 22:28), incest (Dt. 27:20ff), sodomy and bestiality (Lv. 18:22ff, 20:13ff), disobedience of religious authority (Dt. 17:8-13) and, of course, murder (Ex. 21:13; Nm. 35:16ff; Dt. 19:11ff), among others.

Jesus Teaches Mercy

Jesus reveals to us the ways of God. Perhaps the essence of his message is captured in his quotation of the prophet Hosea on the occasion of the call of Matthew: "Go and learn the meaning of the words, 'It is mercy I desire and not sacrifice'" (Mt. 9:13). Here we catch a glimpse of the development that has taken place within the scriptures themselves. Now the people of God can understand that it is not punishment of sinners but mercy toward them that best corresponds with the holiness and justice of God. Indeed, as Paul teaches, the justice of God is shown precisely in his gift of Jesus to a sinful people. This more profound understanding of God's ways, that his mercy is his justice, was only revealed in the life and teachings of Christ.

Tennessee Bishops, *Origins*, June 14, 1984.

These offenses should be regarded with the utter seriousness which their gravity demands. But the prescription of stoning (or in some cases burning) the offender to death must be seen in historical and theological perspective. Rabbis have concluded that the law, the Torah, leaves open the possibility of more appropriate punishment in new historical circumstances.

The fact that we speak from distinctively Christian commitment and perspective in no way lessens our gratitude for the wisdom of our Jewish colleagues on the subject of capital punishment. We remain in dialogue and in harmony with them.

The Gospels

For Christians, however, there are significant insights to be gained from the gospels on the subject.

At the time of his own execution Jesus spoke words of forgiveness, imputing to his executioners a lack of knowledge, of understanding (Lk. 23:34). There can be no doubt that the execution was unfair, but the forgiveness prayed for by our Lord extended beyond that to the violence of the act itself. Jesus offered his disciples an alternative to violence, a new way: "You have heard the commandment, 'An eye for an eye, a tooth for a tooth,' But what I say to you is: Offer no resistance to injury. When a person strikes you on the right cheek, turn and offer him the other" (Mt. 5:38-40).

Jesus enunciated another theme of relevance to the present discussion: God's boundless love for every person, regardless of human merit or worthiness. This love was especially visible in his ministry to outcasts, in his acceptance of sinners and in his parables. In his parables of the workers in the vineyard (Mt. 20:1-14) and the prodigal son (Lk. 15:11-32), God deals with undeserving people not out of strict justice, but out of limitless love and mercy.

Need for Reconciliation

Another emphasis of the Gospels is the imperative of reconciliation. Reconciliation, in Matthew 5, becomes the point of connection between ethics and worship. "If you bring your gift to the altar and there recall that your brother has anything against you, leave your gift at the altar, go first to be reconciled to your brother, and then come and offer your gift" (Mt. 5:23-26).

In the Gospel according to John, Chapter 8, verses 3-11, there is a remarkable story that conveys the force of Jesus' attitude toward what was, in his day, a capital crime. A woman was about to be stoned to death in the temple courtyard for adultery. Jesus asked her religiously orthodox accusers which of them was without sin and invited that one to cast the first stone.

The seventh chapter of Matthew opens with a warning that we ourselves are subject to a judgment as severe as the judgment we impose upon others. The point is not that there is no final judgment on human sin and error, but that the ultimate judgment rests with God (Mt. 25:31-46). St. Paul warns, "Vengeance is mine, says the Lord. I will repay" (Rom. 12:19).

Jesus was not casual about iniquity nor "soft on crime." What he did was to shift the locus of judgment in these matters to a higher court: a court where there is absolute knowlege of the evidence, of good deeds and of evil, of faith and of the works of faith, of things private and things public—a court in which there is both wrath and tenderness, both law and grace.

Responsibility to Victims

The state bears responsibility for the protection of its citizens and merits our fullest support in the exercise of that function. The complexities and ambiguities of violent criminal behavior, especially its psychological and sociological origins, lie beyond our present capacity to understand them. Nonetheless, we believe that society has the right and the duty to prevent such behavior including, in some cases, the right to impose terms of lifetime imprisonment.

A belief in God's love as redemptive and restorative compels us to seek even for those who have taken a life the opportunity for a personal transaction of penitence, restoration and a new

89

beginning—even though imprisoned. The institutionalized taking of human life prevents, eclipses and foreshortens the potential fulfillment of the commitment on our part to seek the redemption and reconciliation of the offender.]

The wrongdoer bears responsibility to God for the infinitely valuable life of the victim and for the suffering of the family and friends of the victim. The term of indebtedness on the part of a convicted offender is lifelong. During imprisonment the offender has certain duties to God, among them to seek religious counsel and the grace of the sacraments; to participate willingly in therapeutic and rehabilitative activities; to pray regularly for those against whom the offense has been an injury; to practice restitution, however inadequate or symbolic, as a serious attempt toward reconciliation with the person to whom he has caused a life of suffering.

Christians Must Oppose Capital Punishment

[We believe that abolition of the death penalty is most consonant with the example of Jesus, who both taught and practiced the forgiveness of injustice and who came "to give his life as a ransom for many" (Mk. 10:45). In this regard we may point to the reluctance which those early Christians who accepted capital punishment as a legitimate practice in civil society felt about the participation of Christians in such an institution and to the unwillingness of the church to accept into the ranks of its ministers those who had been involved in the infliction of capital punishment. There is and has been a certain sense that even in those cases where serious justifications can be offered for the necessity of taking life, those who are identified in a special way with Christ should refrain from taking life.

We believe that this should be taken as an indication of the deeper desires of the church as it responds to the story of God's redemptive and forgiving love as manifest in the life of his Son.

US Bishops, *Origins*, November 1980.\

The fundamental issue here is the restoration of peace: peace in the hearts of the broken, peace in the hearts of the violent, peace in the hearts of all members of the community. This peace rests in the confidence that God will judge fairly and mercifully. It removes from the hands of those who govern the stain of what is at best a morally ambiguous death policy. It constitutes, in our opinion, a constructive venture in faith toward that peace which surpasses all human understanding and which the world can neither give nor take away.

[It is our conclusion that the use of capital punishment. . . must be discontinued. We seriously question that it does any good, and we are deeply convinced that it does a great deal of harm. Our principal objection to it lies in what we believe to be its immorality. Just as the state has its rights and duties, we believe we have the right and duty to speak, after careful deliberation, on that which we believe to be immoral.⟩

Distinguishing Between Fact and Opinion

This activity is designed to help develop the basic reading and thinking skill of distinguishing between fact and opinion. Consider the following statement as an example: "Some states do not allow the death penalty to be imposed for any kind of crime." This statement is a fact; its truth can be checked easily in many books and articles. But consider another statement about capital punishment: "The death penalty contaminates everybody—from the judge or jury to the executioner and the criminal—who participates in it." This statement is clearly an expressed opinion.

When investigating controversial issues it is important that one be able to distinguish between statements of fact and statements of opinion. It is also important to recognize that not all statements of fact are true. They may appear to be true, but some are based on inaccurate or false information. For this activity, however, we are concerned with understanding the difference between those statements which appear to be factual and those which appear to be based primarily on opinion.

Most of the following statements are taken from the viewpoints in this chapter. Consider each statement carefully. *Mark O for any statement you believe is an opinion or interpretation of facts. Mark F for any statement you believe is a fact.*

If you are doing this activity as a member of a class or group, compare your answers with those of other class or group members. Be able to defend your answers. You may discover that others will come to different conclusions than you. Listening to the reasons others present for their answers may give you valuable insights in distinguishing between fact and opinion.

If you are reading this book alone, ask others if they agree with your answers. You too will find this interaction very valuable.

O = opinion
F = fact

92

1. A punishment that inflicts harm on the person can hardly be good or moral if it is purposeless.
2. The execution of an offender is the most certain way to incapacitate him or eliminate his further offenses against society.
3. Society is a moral unity; an offense by one harms the well-being of all.
4. Capital punishment overcompensates for the violation of justice and moral unity created by serious crimes.
5. Capital punishment is imposed merely to gratify an unworthy desire for revenge.
6. Retribution gives the feeling of justice that is indispensable if the law is to be socially supported.
7. Capital punishment expresses the extreme disapproval of the community by imposing its most extreme punishment.
8. Prohibiting the death penalty demonstrates a misguided concern for the criminals instead of for the victims of crime and their families.
9. Society must be protected from criminals and the death penalty is the way to do that.
10. When a person has raped and murdered a child, that person has relinquished the right to live.
11. Capital punishment undermines belief in the inherent worth of human life.
12. Many people think that by executing some criminals, we will deter others.
13. Capital punishment serves to remind us of the majesty of the moral order that is embodied in our law, and of the terrible consequences of its breach.
14. The Supreme Court has ruled that individual states may choose to impose or prohibit the death penalty.
15. State-sanctioned executions expose the violence and injustice that are in us all.
16. It is automatic to file appeals when a criminal is sentenced to death.
17. It is not easy to ward off bitterness and the desire for retaliation when someone has injured us or our loved ones.

Periodical Bibliography

The following list of periodical articles deals with the subject matter of this chapter.

America	"Pornography of Death," April 21, 1984.
Suzanne Belote	"A Life on Death Row," *The Catholic Worker*, January/February 1985.
David Brudnov	"Death Penalty: Sometimes the People Are Right," *The Washington Times*, January 13, 1983.
David Clarke	"Response to Retribution: Impressions at the Site of an Execution," *Network Newsletter*, November/December 1984.
Marie Deans	"A Survivior's View of Murder," *The Witness*, April 1985.
Joe M. Doss	"Capital Punishment: Morality and the Law," *The Witness*, April 1985.
Jim Edwards	"Today, Murderers Are Wrongly Portrayed As Victims of Society," *The Union Leader*, April 9, 1985.
Jeffrey Hart	"Speed Up the Executions," *The Union Leader*, April 12, 1984.
Joseph Ingle	"It's Not the Dying," *The Other Side*, March 1985.
Eric Jorstad	"Church Conflict Over Capital Punishment," *The Christian Century*, July 3/10, 1985.
National Review	"Death Penalty Update," May 4, 1984.
The Progressive	"The Murderers Among Us," January 1984.
Marshall Shelley	"The Death Penalty: Two Sides of a Growing Issue," *Christianity Today*, March 2, 1984.
Karl Spence	"Crime and Punishment," *National Review*, September 16, 1983.
Douglas Sturm	"Personal Perspective: 2 (The Ultimate Sanction)," *Christianity and Crisis*, April 15, 1985.
Ernest van den Haag	"For the Death Penalty," *The New York Times*, October 17, 1983.

Does the Death Penalty Deter Murder?

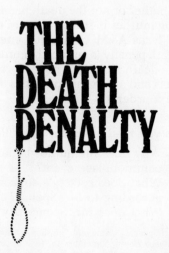

"Even when they were a rarity, executions had served a purpose . . . . The most influential study . . . concludes that a substantial deterrent effect has been observed."

The Death Penalty Deters Murder

Karl Spence

Whether or not the death penalty can deter others from committing murder is still an issue of contention. Karl Spence, a student at Texas A&M University, cites studies to prove that when the death penalty is enforced, murder decreases, and conversely, when the death penalty is not enforced, murder increases. From these facts and others, he concludes that the death penalty deters would-be murderers.

As you read, consider the following questions:

1. Why does the author believe that murder has become a commonplace event?
2. What does society's concern for victims of crime require, according to Mr. Spence?
3. What does Mr. Spence say that society must do?

Karl Spence, "Crime and Punishment," excerpted from pages 1140, 1142, 1144, 1161, *National Review,* September 16, 1983. Reprinted with permission from National Review Inc., 150 East 35th Street, New York, NY 10016.

Fifteen years ago crime was, apart from the Vietnam War, our country's most divisive political problem. Crime was on the rise, but our political leaders and opinion-makers could not agree on why, or how much, or who was to blame, or what should or could be done about it. J. Edgar Hoover had started the controversy in the early 1960s with a series of warnings that rising crime threatened the well-being of the nation. Hoover's opponents in academia and elsewhere charged that he was crying wolf. There had been, they insisted, no substantial change in crime rates. As the decade wore on, however, it became apparent that a serious crime problem had developed and finally demanded attention.

Mass Murder Common

Robbery increased sevenfold in two decades, and the transitive verb to mug entered the language. Mass murder became so common that multiple killings frequently were reported on the inside pages of the newspaper. In fact, the most horrifying aspect of this situation is the indifference with which it is now viewed by the nation. Skid-row drunks are tortured to death, young women are raped and strangled, whole families are murdered in their beds, while the rest of us go on about our business. By the fall of 1976, when an elderly couple in New York City were robbed and tortured twice in their own apartment and then hanged themselves, saying they didn't want "to live in fear anymore," very few people noticed. The slaughter and plunder of American citizens had become a basic part of the American way of life.

Still, there is no consensus as to the cause of this rise in violent, predatory crime, and, therefore, no consensus as to a solution. Suggestions range from eliminating poverty to making punishment more certain and more severe. Those alternatives unfortunately are regarded as being mutually exclusive, and it is widely held that of the two only the former is "enlightened" and morally acceptable. But we must learn to look for the suppression of crime, not as a result of social and economic progress, but as a precondition of it. We must also realize that eliminating poverty would eliminate crime only if a majority of criminals acted out of necessity. In fact, most commit their crimes because they choose to do so, and they must be dealt with by other than economic means.

One of the methods by which we "deal" with crime is to erect a great array of defenses, such as electronic security systems at airports and banks, neighborhood watch programs, multiple locks on apartment doors, and attempts at more comprehensive gun control. These, alas, are all stop-gap measures, aimed at symptoms only. They put the nation into a permanent state of siege and imply that the only way we can be sure that our neighbor will not attack us is to make it impossible for him to do so. This fearful distrust, so destructive to all feeling of community, is perhaps the most evil consequence of our failure to control crime.

97

Police across the nation have blamed the Supreme Court for the bulk of the crime increase, saying that the broadening of suspects' rights under the Warren Court hampered them to such an extent that an ensuing crime wave was inevitable. Many would dispute that, but it is clear that the governing image of the Warren reforms—that of the solitary and helpless individual overwhelmed by the vast resources of the state—is not reflected in current reality, in which it is the police and the courts that are being overwhelmed (despite the backtracking by the Burger Court in the last year or so). Yet no amount of reform making it easier to obtain convictions will be of any use if the resulting punishments are so light that, far from deterring others by their example, they do not dissuade even the convict himself from resuming his criminal career.

Bill DeOre, *The Dallas Morning News*, reprinted with permission.

So we arrive at the need for punishment, and since we are especially concerned with violent crime, our remedy will include capital punishment. Here is the point of greatest controversy: To a sizable minority of Americans, the death penalty is one alternative that is unacceptable to a civilized society. Many people hate the idea of executions as much as they hate those crimes for which execution has been the standard punishment. Before we pursue that course of action, then, their objections must be met.

[One] basic argument [has] been raised against capital punishment: . . . it is not an effective deterrent. . . .

If the death penalty has no deterrent value, theoretical justifications of it may frequently be overridden by the desirability of showing mercy to the convict and attempting his rehabilitation. But if executions do have deterrent value, opposition to them becomes pernicious, dooming many more people than it saves. Predictably, opponents of capital punishment approach this question of fact and come away with conclusions to fit their preconceptions. But it is here that the argument against capital punishment is weakest.

We ought to understand that the deterrence question is at present not one of proof but of possibility. . . . Our concern for future victims requires absolute *certainty* that crime cannot be reduced, in any degree, by executions, of whatever scope, before it will allow us to forbear proceeding *to* the proof, which is to execute murderers. Can such certainty intelligently be maintained? I suggest not.

The statistical support for the belief that executions do not deter (primarily, Thorsten Sellin's 1959 study, which covered the years 1920-1955) deals with an era in which death for murder was the exception rather than the rule, and the no-deterrence argument assumes that for humanitarian reasons such will always be the case. Declining to consider what might happen to the murder rate if executions increased, abolitionists in the mid-Sixties confidently predicted that nothing untoward would ensue if executions ceased entirely. As the chart on this page shows, their expectations were disappointed. It began to appear that even when they were a rarity, executions had served a purpose, and reassessments were forthcoming. While some abolitionists try to face down the results of their disastrous experiment, and still argue to the contrary, the most influential . . . study—Isaac Ehrlich's "The Deterrent Effect of Capital Punishment". . .—concludes that a substantial deterrent effect has been observed.

	Capital Punishment	
Year	**Executions**	**Murders**
1957	65	8,060
1958	49	8,220
1959	49	8,580
1960	56	9,140
1961	42	8,600
1962	47	8,400
1963	21	8,500
1964	15	9,250
1965	7	9,850
1966	1	10,920

1967	2	12,090
1968	0	13,650
1969	0	14,590
1970	0	15,810
1971	0	17,630
1972	0	18,520
1973	0	19,510
1974	0	20,600
1975	0	20,510
1976	0	18,780
1977	1	19,120
1978	0	19,560
1979	2	21,460
1980	0	23,040
1981	1	22,520

Ehrlich's evidence and the Supreme Court's approval notwithstanding, authorities around the country continue to stay their hands, fearful of the "bloodbath" if the hundreds of persons under sentence of death were executed in rapid order. In the meantime, a real bloodbath goes on unabated. In six months, more Americans are murdered than have died by execution in this entire century.

The experts tell us that that's the way it is and the way it will be. But what if we *used* the death penalty, and not just for the most extremely heinous crimes, but as a standard punishment? Can we hold ourselves guiltless if we do not? By no means. Until we begin to fight crime in earnest, every person who dies at a criminal's hands is a victim of our inaction.

J. Edgar Hoover, who seized the crime wave of his day and bore it down beneath the sheer weight of his activity, once said, "Crime is a dangerous, cancerous condition which, if not curbed, will soon eat at the very vitals of the country." Today, we see the decay of our inner cities, we read of tragedy and outrage until we are numb, and many of us have felt the sickening touch of brutality in our own lives.

Society must once again assume the right and accept the duty of exacting retribution.

"That the death penalty is a failure as a deterrent to murder has been demonstrated in many ways. That it is a success as an incentive to murder . . . is increasingly clear."

The Death Penalty Incites Murder

Louis Joylon West

Louis Joylon West is psychiatrist-in-chief, professor, and chairman of the Department of Psychiatry and Biobehavioral Sciences at the University of California, Los Angeles (UCLA) Medical Center. He is also the director of the Neuropsychiatric Institute of UCLA. In the following viewpoint, Mr. West points to his experience in treating prisoners on death row to support his argument that the death penalty incites murder.

As you read, consider the following questions:

1. Why are there more homicides in death penalty states, according to the author?
2. Why does the author believe that some murders are attempts at suicide on the part of the criminal?
3. Why, according to Mr. West, are most people not incited to commit murder?

Louis Joylon West, MD, "Psychiatric Reflections on the Death Penalty," *American Journal of Orthopsychiatry*, Vol. 45 No. 4. Copyright by the American Orthopsychiatric Association, Inc. Reprinted with permission.

I have come to believe that thoughtful persons who study the subject objectively will be likely to arrive at the firm conclusion that the death penalty should be totally and permanently abolished. True, we are shocked at the horrors that violent criminals are capable of perpetrating. We become filled with concern and sympathy for victims, their families and survivors. We ask ourselves, "Suppose *my* daughter were raped and butchered?" The very question fills us with outrage, and acquaints us not only with our own potentialities for vengeful murder, but with the type of passion that moves both lynch mobs and (in various disguises) a violence-plagued citizenry in desiring both protection and retribution.

But the prisoner convicted of a capital crime is confined. He is protected from vengeful personal retaliation. Society is now also safe from him. Should society nevertheless exterminate him, deliberately and righteously? When scholars consider this question in depth, the weight of the evidence makes itself felt. It moves us to the viewpoint probably shared not only by most wardens and governors, but by the majority of criminologists, jurists, philosophers, and those social and behavioral scientists who have surveyed the same ground. . . .

Capital Punishment Breeds Murder

Of all the arguments against the death penalty. . .there is one that is perhaps both least understood and most paradoxical: *Capital punishment breeds murder.* Philosophers and social scientists have long contended that the legal extermination of human beings in any society generates a profound tendency among the citizens to accept killing as a solution to human problems. In fact there are convincing data cited elsewhere to show that around the time and place of a well-published execution, the murder rate is quite likely to go up, rather than down.

No matter how ultimate the death penalty as a solution may seem, or how rarely it is employed, its official existence or acceptance in the law symbolizes the fact that it is permissible—even desirable—to resolve issues by murder; it is only necessary to define the criteria for justification. Thus, Camus steadfastly held that it would be necessary for mankind to eliminate the death penalty before we could ever hope to eliminate war. He took pains to point out that no nation which had wholly and permanently abolished capital punishment ever started a war.

But I am convinced that there is an even more specific way in which the death penalty breeds murder. It becomes more than a symbol. It becomes a promise, a contract, a covenant between society and certain (by no means rare) warped mentalities who are moved to kill as part of a self-destructive urge. These murders are discovered by the psychiatric examiner to be, consciously or unconsciously, perpetrated in an attempt to commit *suicide* by committing *homicide*. It only works if the perpetrator believes he will be executed for his crime. I believe this to be a significant reason for the tendency to find proportionally more homicides in death penalty states than in those without it. I even know of cases where the murderer left an abolitionist state deliberately to commit a meaningless murder in an executionist state, in the hope thereby of forcing society to destroy him. But there are many instances far less elaborate, and quite obvious not only to the psychiatrist but to any sensible observer.

"Just Tired of Living"

For example, in 1965 an Oklahoma truck driver parked to have lunch in a Texas roadside cafe. A total stranger—a farmer from nearby—walked through the door and blew him in half with a shotgun. When the police finally disarmed the farmer and asked why he had murdered the trucker, he replied, "I was just tired of living."

In 1964, Howard Otis Lowery, a life-term convict in an Oklahoma prison, formally requested a judge to send him to the electric chair after a District Court jury found him sane following a prison escape and a spree of violence. He said that if he could not get the death penalty from one jury he would get it from another, and complained that officials had failed to live up to an agreement to give him death in the electric chair when he pleaded guilty to a previous murder charge in 1961.

Murders Increase

We believe that the death penalty actually increases the potential of murder in this country. . . .

The truly psychotic in this society—the John Wayne Gacys of Illinois, the Richard Specks, the Sons of Sam, the Charles Mansons, those people whose behavior is so outside of our comprehension that they have to be seen as aberrant. Not only are such persons not deterred by capital punishment, but may in fact flock around it like moths around a flame.

Michael Kroll, testimony before the Senate Judiciary Committee, May 1, 1981.

Another murderer, James French, asked for the death penalty after he wantonly killed a motorist who gave him a ride while French was hitch-hiking through Oklahoma in 1958. However, French was foiled by his court-appointed public defense attorney who made a deal with the prosecutor, pleaded his client guilty and got him a life sentence instead of the requested execution. French was outraged. He had thought the guilty plea would bring certain execution. Repeated letters to the governor demanding execution or a new trial were ignored. Finally, three years later, in the State Penitentiary at McAlester, French strangled his cell-mate. This was a deliberate, premeditated slaying, without any known motive except to get himself executed. In fact that was the motive given by French himself. For this final murder French was convicted three times. (There were two successful appeals by public defenders for new trials on technical grounds, much to French's irritation.) He was declared legally sane and sentenced to death each time. This sentence he deliberately invited in well-organized, literate epistles to the courts, and in provocative, taunting challenges to judges and jurors. During a psychiatric examination in 1965, French admitted to me that he had seriously attempted suicide several times in the past but always "chickened out" at the last minute. His basic (and obviously abnormal) motive in murdering his inoffensive cell-mate was to force the State to deliver to him the electrocution to which he felt entitled and which he deeply desired. French was the only man who was executed in the United States during 1966. He had successfully forced the State of Oklahoma to fulfill its contract to reward murder with murder. If Oklahoma had *not* had the death penalty, it is likely that both of the men murdered by James French would still be alive.

Effects of the Death Penalty

Many other examples may be found in which the promise of the death penalty consciously or unconsciously invites violence. Sellin reviewed a number of them. Wertham's analysis of Robert Irwin, who attempted suicide by murder, is a classic. Some who seek execution even confess to somebody else's murder. For example, in 1966 Joseph Shay, in Miami, admitted that he had falsely confessed to an unsolved murder "because I wanted to die" (cited in various local and national news reports). The intimate connection between murder and suicide has been discussed by Alexander, Menninger, Zilboorg, and other psychiatrists. West noted that in England nearly half of all murders are followed by serious suicidal attempts, of which two-thirds succeed. In other words, about one-third of all murderers in England die by suicide. In Denmark, where there has been no death penalty for generations (and where, of course, the murder rate is far lower than ours), 40% of all murderers subsequently commit suicide.

That the death penalty is a failure as a deterrent to murder has been demonstrated in many ways. That it is a success as an incentive to murder, either generally (through its influence as symbolic representation of the acceptability of killing) or specifically in cases like those described above, is increasingly clear. It makes it easier to understand why, for example, in the year following the widely publicized re-establishment of capital punishment in formerly abolitionist Oregon in 1920, that state's homicide rate nearly doubled.

104

In light of the general trend toward abolition of capital punishment in the Western World, and of the successful experience of Michigan (abolitionist since 1847) and a dozen other states for many years, why is there now such great desire among the American people to see the death penalty restored? Some of the current pressure undoubtedly comes from the steadily rising rate of violent crime which has accompanied the population explosion, the acute problems of urbanization, the easy availability of handguns, and other factors. A number of unusually horrible and highly publicized murders, like those by Charles Manson and his followers, have also been cited as causative. (These were committed, one should note, *before* capital punishment was abolished in California; the death penalty did not protect Manson's victims.)

Some Demand the Death Penalty

There have been studies which indicate. . .that precisely the spectacle of State-imposed death may increase the homicide rate. First of all, it may do this because it may stimulate certain people who identify not with the person who is being killed but with the State which is doing the killing. It may stimulate them to feel that if they have a grievance that they can go out and do the same.

There are many cases which have been documented of people. . .who have death wishes, who have a suicidal tendency, but they do not want to kill themselves; they prefer to go out and kill somebody else and even demand the death penalty.

Vincent McGee, testimony before the Senate Judiciary Committee, May 1, 1981.

Nor did it protect the eight student nurses slaughtered in executionist Illinois by Richard Speck, who had just left abolitionist Michigan, where he ignored similar access to nurses and showed no signs of violence.) Of course pressure is also due to the reiteration by prominent public figures (some of whom should know better) that capital punishment is a successful deterrent to violent crime and is needed to protect the community. But many people are remarkably quick to accept such arguments, and peculiarly resistant to any arguments to the contrary. . . .

Most People Don't Murder

It is not fear of retaliation ("a death for a death") that keeps most normal people from murder. Rather it is a healthy appreciation for the value of human life, the capacity for empathy with others, and the sense of belonging to a society in which persons have meaning. It should be no surprise to find that those states and counties which have long since abolished the death penalty have in their statutes also reflected many other humane considerations.

105

This may also contribute to the persistent findings that such states and nations have fewer capital crimes, even without the death penalty, than do comparable neighbors that have retained capital punishment; and that indeed the abolitionist society is likely to be generally somewhat less violent than the executionist one. . . .

The struggle to eliminate the penalty of death is a continuing one. The forces of progress are at work, not only in medicine, but in other professions as well. Working together, the many professional and learned societies of the United States could do much to secure the final and permanent abolition of the death penalty in our country. This would be a signal victory in the never-ending struggle to create progress through the exercise of reason in human affairs.

"Only when committing murder is tantamount to committing suicide will the carnage abate."

More Executions Will Deter Murder

Neil Bright

Neil Bright is a member of Young Americans for Freedom and is currently working on his Ph.D. in political science. In the following viewpoint, he argues that the deterrent value of the death penalty is lost because of its rare application. The only way to show the death penalty as a deterrent is to execute more murderers.

As you read, consider the following questions:

1. According to the author, how are death row inmates a confirmation that deterrence works?
2. What is essential for any punishment to act as a deterrent, according to Mr. Bright?
3. What human instinct does Mr. Bright say the death penalty confronts?

Neil Bright, "Beyond a Reasonable Doubt," *New Guard*, Summer 1982. Reprinted with permission.

The controversy over capital punishment is unending. Like high school debaters, both sides cite countless studies and infinite statistics as the blood of innocents continues to mingle with the tears of those who mourn. Does the death penalty deter murder? No one seems to know. Despite mountains of data, it still is uncertain whether ending a murderer's life will save anyone else's. What *is* beyond doubt is that our present system of crime and punishment is inadequate. The more than twenty thousand yearly murder victims bear silent witness to this reality.

What is difficult to demonstrate on a societal level is often easier to confirm on an individual one. In some homicides, the decision to pull the trigger or plunge the knife is calmly made. In at least some ways it is a rational choice. Why is this necessary? What are my chances for success? How shall I cover my tracks? Because most people dance to tunes of self-preservation, capital punishment which is swift and certain will threaten to silence the music. Only when committing murder is tantamount to committing suicide will the carnage abate.

The best place to observe the deterrent value of capital punishment is in some ways the most unlikely. It is death row. It is among those who were *not* deterred by the most severe of all penalties that its benefit is most clearly seen. It is on death row that those who have taken life fight to preserve their own. With few exceptions, convicted murderers do not go gently into the night. They exhaust every legal avenue in an effort to save for themselves what they cruelly ended for others. If being so close to eternity did not invoke overwhelming fear, why then would men fight for breath as little more than caged animals?

Effects of Non-Use

Critics point to rising homicide rates as proof that capital punishment does not deter capital offense. Perhaps the reason there hasn't been a murder reduction since the death penalty was ruled constitutional has less to do with the punishment than with its lack of use. It is essential that gas chambers and electric chairs be more than idle threats. In order to be effective, they must serve society not as little-used artifacts of a barbaric past but as active deterrents to the barbarism of the present.

The belief in immortality and that adversity is for others is not limited to the law-abiding and the naive. Murderers also visit fairy tale places where all works out in the end. With less than ten executions occurring in the last ten years, it is easy for those with murderous potential to believe they will evade eternal payment. The deterrent value of any punishment is directly related to its frequency of use. It shouldn't be assumed that this axiom applies any less to murder than it does for shoplifting. As long as the death penalty remains cruel but unusual, the good and the unlucky will continue to die young.

Critics fault the death penalty on grounds that in a fallible legal system an innocent may be wrongly executed. Capital punishment itself has been condemned for its lack of perfection. An impossible standard is set and when there is no guarantee that such a standard can be reached, objection is the result. There can be, of course, no assurance that the ultimate miscarriage of justice will never occur. The only certainty is that innocents are presently being "executed" with increasing frequency. Something must be done. There is far greater chance that many will be justly saved as a result of capital punishment than a single individual wrongly killed because of it.

The Abolitionist's Myth

Myth: "The death penalty doesn't deter crime."

Don't believe it. Kidnapping was almost a national epidemic until it was made punishable by death. Then it almost disappeared. And as the number of executions in this country declined, the number of murders went up. If the number of executions ever started going up again, you'd see the number of murders decline.

Mike Royko, *Chicago Sun-Times*, September 1983.

Mistaken execution, however, is not the only concern of those opposing capital punishment. Instead of simply arguing the imperfection of the courts, critics point as well to the imperfection within the system. A disproportionate number of convicted killers are members of minority groups. Because the poor black or Hispanic is unable to hire lawyers as skilled as more affluent white, the end result is a certain ticket to oblivion. One would expect those complaining the loudest would racially mirror those so close to the edge. But that is often not the case. Critics of capital punishment frequently reside far from the misery spawning a murder every twenty-three minutes. Of the 65 percent of those favoring the death penalty, many are neither wealthy nor white. This should not be surprising. Minority group members have the most to gain from capital punishment. It is for them that a violent and criminal end is most often reserved.

A Grim Necessity

The ivory towers are full of those far from the savagery of the streets. With knee-jerk certainty, they attack the death penalty believing it will brutalize the very society advocates say it will protect. It is a natural reaction. Those mandated to pass such laws and those doubting their effect are not murderers. To them, any life, even that of a convicted killer, is sacrosanct. Those objecting to capital punishment would rather not consent to its grim necessity or be reminded of man's darker side. There is a dual quality to human nature. We are capable of all that is progress, beauty and love. But the beast also walks among us and it is he who must be destroyed.

Extinction Must Be Assured

The instinctual desire for self-preservation will reach killers where morality and life sentences can never venture. It must become clear to latent murderers that extinction in a chair or at the end of a rope is assured. The terror of death for potential killers outside prison walls must resemble the panic of convicted killers within. The will to survive must be placed in direct opposition to the will to slaughter. For years, innocents have lived with the fear of death dictated by an accelerating murder rate. The time has come for would-be slayers to become acquainted with that same companion.

"Any deterrent effect of the death penalty in any case would be no more justification than the arguably even greater deterrent effect of prolonged torture or burning at the stake on the murder rate."

Deterrence Cannot Justify Executions

Henry Schwarzschild

Henry Schwarzschild is the director of the Capital Punishment project of the American Civil Liberties Union in New York City. The American Civil Liberties Union opposes the imposition of the death penalty. In the following viewpoint, Mr. Schwarzschild argues that the deterrence theory is irrelevant. The argument is not whether or not the death penalty can deter, but that state-sanctioned executions are immoral and inhumane under any circumstances.

As you read, consider the following questions:

1. What two arguments does the author say are most commonly used to support the death penalty?
2. Does Mr. Schwarzschild believe these arguments are justified? Why or why not?
3. How does Mr. Schwarzschild believe the death penalty should be viewed?

Henry Schwarzschild, "A Social and Moral Atrocity," *ABA Journal*, April 1985. Reprinted with permission from the ABA Journal, The Lawyer's Magazine.

Killing human beings in order to solve social problems is deeply uncivilized. There are now almost 1,500 people on death row in this country. We sentence people to death additionally at the rate of about 250 a year. Since the Supreme Court's *Gregg* decision in 1976, we have done almost 40 executions, well over half of them in the past 15 months. The pace is quickening ominously. This country is about to become one of the world's large-scale executioners, in company with the People's Republic of China, the Soviet Union, South Africa and Iran. That is a dispiriting reputation to earn and melancholy company to keep.

Who Lives, Who Dies

The death penalty is the state's arrogation of God-like wisdom (or totalitarian power) to decide who should live and who should die. People who would not dream of letting the government dictate what morning newspaper to read or what spouse to marry seem to have no problem with letting the government decide whom to kill. And this in a century in which we have seen governments shed rivers of blood—in wars, revolutions and extermination camps, by militias and death squads and sheriffs—always justifying their lethal fury by the benefits the killings would bring to the rest of the society. Governments, we might have learned by now, are inappropriate agencies to select some people to be killed.

The death penalty is usually defended on two grounds: that it is useful and that it is just.

The argument of social utility rests primarily on the case for deterrence—the claim that the availability of capital punishment or the carrying out of executions diminishes the incidence of violent crime. The evidence for that proposition is essentially nil, intuition and common sense notwithstanding. The evidence for the contrary is overwhelming. By and large, people who commit the heinous crimes for which they might get sentenced to death either expect to get away with it, in which case the severity of the threatened sanction makes no difference, or they act under pressures of the moment—whether internal (lust, greed, fear, hatred, or under the influence of alcohol, drugs, or psychic pathology) or external (fear of imminent discovery or arrest, or expectation of being themselves shot or the like). They will commit the crime heedless of the consequences, in which case the remote possibility of the death sentence does not restrain their actions.

Long-Term Imprisonment Enough

If a crime is unpremeditated, it is impossible to imagine how any punishment can be a deterrent. If it is premeditated and if severe punishment indeed can deter, then long-term imprisonment is severe enough to cause any rational person not to commit violent crimes. Irrational crimes, it goes without saying, are immune to deterrent threats.

If, on the other hand, usefulness is thought to lie in the exemplary effect of the death penalty—in establishing dramatically that the society will not tolerate behavior so unforgiveably destructive as murder—then there arises the unanswerable question of how a society can teach that killing people is wrong by itself committing spectacular premeditated violent homicide.

Deterrence Not Justified

Any deterrent effect of the death penalty in any case would be no more justification than the arguably even greater deterrent effect of prolonged torture or burning at the stake on the murder rate or the introduction of maiming as a penalty for burglary. The objection here is on grounds of fundamental decency, and arguments of usefulness will not avail against those.

That the death penalty continues to be imposed with extraordinary arbitrariness and irrationality is conveniently illustrated by a . . . case in which one co-defendant was executed while his precisely equally guilty fellow offender will be eligible for parole in about seven years, and by another in which the triggerman got a term of imprisonment while the non-triggerman was executed.

Murderous Crimes Are Unplanned

The U.S. Supreme Court has noted that there is no conclusive evidence that the death penalty acts as a deterrent. Capital crimes are often impulsive and unplanned, and neither the presence of the death penalty nor the frequency of executions have been shown to have any significant effect on homicide rates. It serves no purpose in the effort to control crime, and must be seen as the most brutal, irrational kind of revenge. In the words of the Michigan Catholic Conference, "It is clear that the root causes of crime lie within society itself, and their effects will not be eliminated by an act of retribution."

The Fellowship of Reconciliation, excerpted from a position statement, c. 1983.

The costs of long-term (even permanent) incarceration turn out to be smaller than the costs of capital trials and extended appeals but it seems hard to justify killing human beings in order to save tax dollars.

Nor has the criminal justice system succeeded in eliminating race, gender or class discrimination from death sentencing. Nonwhites commonly are sentenced to death for crimes for which whites would get a prison sentence. Killers of white victims, moreover, are far more likely to be sentenced to death than those whose victims were non-white.

113

That innocent people will occasionally be executed is a logically necessary inference from human fallibility.

Is the death penalty proper because it is just, irrespective of its usefulness? If that means that the punishment should be like the crime, then by that principle we would rape rapists and torture torturers. A civilized criminal justice system does not use so irrational and unacceptable a mode of selecting punishments. If justice here means that the penalty should be proportional to the crime, then the principle is sound but does not require support for the death penalty. It means, rather, that crimes other than murder should be punished less severely. Capital punishment violates elementary human dignity and human rights and therefore cannot serve the ends of justice.

The death penalty does not deter crime and it is uncivilized in theory and unfair and inequitable in practice. It should be recognized as cruel and unusual punishment, in violation of the Eighth Amendment, and it should be abolished. We shall look back on it ultimately as we now remember chattel slavery: with horror.

"One can't justify the restoration of capital punishment on no more than the theoretical possibility that it has some desirable deterrent effect on the rate of homicide."

Inconclusive Evidence Invalidates the Deterrence Theory

David Bruck

Many studies attempting to prove the deterrent effect of capital punishment have been undertaken. None to date has been able to conclusively demonstrate whether or not the death penalty will deter future murders. In the following viewpoint, David Bruck writes that it is this unprovability that makes the deterrence theory insupportable. As long as this doubt persists, Mr. Bruck argues, society must err on the side of the criminal. David Bruck practices law in Columbia, South Carolina. He writes frequently on the subject of the death penalty.

As you read, consider the following questions:

1. Why does the author find the deterrence theory unlikely?
2. What risks does Mr. Bruck say make the deterrence arguments unjustified?
3. How is the criminal viewed by deterrence proponents, according to the author?

David I. Bruck, "The Death Penalty in the United States" revised draft, March 9, 1985. Reprinted with the author's permission.

The most commonly-cited justification for capital punishment is that it is a deterrent to murder. Supporters of the death penalty assert that the threat of execution serves to save innocent lives by dissuading individuals who would choose to commit murder but for the danger that they might be required to forfeit their own lives.

Those who hold this view say that it rests on common sense. Death, the argument goes, is the most severe punishment. It therefore follows that the threat of being punished by death will serve as a more effective deterrent than any other punishment. But this deterrence argument rests on a number of doubtful assumptions. First, it assumes that people decide to commit murder only after first making a cool calculation of the pros and cons—including possible punishments. Second, in order to be deterred by an especially severe punishment, the potential murderer must anticipate that he will be caught, tried and convicted: if he doesn't expect to be arrested, not even crucifixion or boiling in oil would be any more of a deterrent than imprisonment, since he's not planning on being punished at all. Finally, since murder is almost invariably punished by long terms of imprisonment even where the death penalty is not available, the death penalty will not have any *superior* deterrent effect to imprisonment unless there are people who wouldn't be willing to risk execution, but who would commit murder if they could be sure that they would "merely" have to spend the next one, two or three decades in prison.

Deterrence Argument Unlikely

It's conceivable that a few murders are committed after such careful weighing of the possible risks. It is even possible that a handful of potential murderers plan their crimes in the expectation of being caught, and will forge ahead only if they can be assured of a lengthy prison sentence rather than being put to death. But it doesn't seem likely that these circumstances will coincide in any substantial number of instances, and so deter murders which would have been committed but for the death penalty.

During the past twenty-five years, social scientists in the United States and elsewhere have attempted to resolve this debate by examining crime statistics in search of a connection between capital punishment and the rate of homicide. This research has generated a very large body of scholarly literature, but has almost uniformly failed to show any evidence that either the availability or the actual infliction of capital punishment has ever been demonstrated [to act as a deterrent. This] provides strong reason to doubt that executions really save innocent lives, as many of its propoents claim.

The last refuge of those who advance the deterrence argument is to concede that the death penalty's deterrent effect has not been proven. However, they stress, until such an effect is conclusively *disproven*, the risk of error should be resolved in favor of the innocent lives that might be protected by executions, rather than by sparing the lives of convicted murderers.

The first thing that's wrong with this argument is that it falsely assumes that murderers are the only people whom the death penalty places at risk. This assumption ignores the danger that innocent defendants might—and over time, almost certainly will—be erroneously executed. And it also overlooks the possibility that the death penalty may under some circumstances serve to *increase* murder rather than decrease it. We simply don't know what effect the undeniably violent symbolism of legal executions may have on mentally ill or embittered individuals. By creating an appearance of social condonation of killing, legal executions may actually incite some murders. This danger is increased by the fact that executions offer potential murderers a degree of fame and notoriety which is not bestowed on criminals sentenced to the oblivion of prison. Even though society may know what it *means* to say when it executes criminals, the message that gets heard may be very different. . . .

Deterrence Is a Delusion

The most common and, in the eyes of proponents, the strongest argument in favor of capital punishment is its deterrent effect. Don't be fooled; the deterrence is all delusion. Criminological and sociological studies show no discernible differences in incidents of capital crime between states that have capital punishment and those that do not, other than what might be accounted for by population numbers, levels of affluence, and other social factors. Even historically the deterrent effect is not able to be proven. The tale is told that when pickpocketing was a capital crime in England, pickpockets would ply their trade at the very foot of the gallows where pickpockets were being hanged. It's probably true.

Paul D. Vincent, *US Catholic*, October 1981.

The magnitudes of each of these risks—the execution of innocent defendants and the incitement of additional murders—can never be accurately measured. But it can't be denied that both of these risks are real. And the existence of such risks means that one can't justify the restoration of capital punishment on no more than the theoretical possibility that it has some desirable deterrent effect on the rate of homicide.

Murderers Are Also Human

In addition, this "why-not-take-a-chance?" approach to capital punishment contains a profound moral flaw, which is that it treats convicted murderers as nonhuman. The argument that even the

117

slightest possibility of a deterrent effect is sufficient justification for the execution of large numbers of convicted murderers assumes that the value of the lives of the convicted prisoners is absolutely nil. Only if the lives of these men and women are worth nothing at all can their executions be justified by so miniscule and purely theoretical a possibility of social benefit through increased deterrence. The killing of human beings on the basis of such doctrinaire reasoning is characteristic of governments which do not represent the fundamental human rights of their own citizens. And it is entirely inconsistent with the attitude of respect for the sanctity of life which supporters of capital punishment in the United States claim as the essential moral basis of the death penalty.

Proponents Cannot Prove Deterrence

In summary, proponents of capital punishment cannot evade the implications of their own inability to demonstrate the deterrent effect of the death penalty. It's just not sufficient to argue that the burden of proof should be on the abolitionist side. Retention of the death penalty poses risks to innocent persons; if supporters of the death penalty think that abolition also poses such risks, they ought to prove that these risks are real rather than imaginary before using them as justification for the methodical killing of human beings.

One additional observation should be made about deterrence. While many supporters of capital punishment will cite its alleged value as a deterrent as the reason for their opinion, there can be little doubt that the most widely-held and important basis of support for capital punishment is not deterrence but the desire "to see justice done"—the motive of retribution. The validity of capital punishment as a way of giving murderers their just punishment is, of course, something which must be determined quite apart from the more narrowly utilitarian question of whether the death penalty has any special deterrent effect. But the two questions can't be so neatly separated, because the use of executions as a deterrent tends to undermine its utility as an instrument of justice. This is so because deterrence, unlike retribution, does not necessarily require that the punishment be just, or that the person being punished actually deserve his punishment. Indeed, deterrence does not even require that the person being punished actually be guilty at all. What is required is only that the condemned person be *perceived* as guilty by the audience—the general public—whose conduct the authorities seek to influence. To the extent that society justifies the death penalty as a deterrent, it is using the condemned man or woman as a sort of human billboard.

This use of human life as a means to an end invariably tends to corrupt and make less accurate the sentencing process in each individual case. To the extent that a sentencing judge or jury is motivated by the desire to punish the defendant *as an example* to others, the sentencer is given a reason to overlook or discount facts about the individual defendant—such as mental illness or retardation, lack of intent to commit murder, or even doubt about his guilt—which might otherwise justify sparing his life. And when such doubts are overlooked or minimized in order to get on with the business of using the defendant as an instrument with which to deter others, both the reliability of the sentencing process and the alleged utility of the death penalty as an instrument of justice are compromised.

"Capital punishment cannot and never will be able to deter all *murderers. But this does not mean for a moment that it won't deter* any *murderers."*

Inconclusive Evidence Does Not Invalidate Deterrence

Frank Carrington

Frank Carrington, author of the following viewpoint, wrote *Neither Cruel nor Unusual*, a well-known book in favor of the death penalty. Mr. Carrington agrees that there is little factual evidence to support the idea that the death penalty is a deterrent to crime. But he does not believe this lack of conclusive support affects the validity of capital punishment. Mr. Carrington asserts that, if used consistently, it could reduce the number of murders committed.

As you read, consider the following questions:

1. Why, according to the author, will we never know how many murders the death penalty has prevented?
2. On the question of deterrence, does Mr. Carrington believe that society should err on the side of the criminal or the victim?
3. The author quotes many criminals on the death penalty. In their opinions, is the death penalty a deterrent? Why or why not?

The question whether future murders will be deterred by the statutory availability *and the application* of the death penalty is far and away the most important argument in the entire controversy. No airtight mathematical proof for or against the deterrent value of capital punishment is available to us now, although scientists on either side of the question have come up with their own analyses and a lively, if rather arcane, debate is raging today.

The basic reason for the lack of certainty in the statistical battle is obvious: it is very difficult to prove a negative conclusively. And that is precisely what the proponents, at least, would have to do. By looking at the number of murders committed while the death penalty was on the books and *enforced*, we can gain some indication of how many killers were obviously *not* deterred (because they committed murder).

However, there is absolutely no way that we can ever know, with any certainty, how many would-be murderers were in fact deterred from killing. By definition, they *were* deterred, they did *not* kill, and therefore we can never know what numbers to enter on that side of the statistical equation. We have some case histories of captured criminals. . .who admitted that the threat of death deterred *them*. But, for the most part, very few people who have not otherwise been embroiled with the law walk into their local precinct house and say to the desk sergeant: "Do you know, I was planning to murder my business partner but the threat of execution deterred me."

As the poet Hyman Barshay has vividly put it:

> The death penalty is a warning, just like a lighthouse throwing its beams out to sea. We hear about shipwrecks, but we do not hear about the ships the lighthouse guides safely on their way. We do not have proof of the number of ships it saves, but we do not tear the lighthouse down. . . .

Most of us, proponent or abolitionist alike, are forced to concede that we will never get a *conclusive* statistical picture of the deterrent effect of the death penalty. We must make do with what data we have, buttressed by a little common sense. . . .

The Threat of Death

The death penalty was dormant in this country from 1967, when the last man was executed, until 1977, when Gary Mark Gilmore paid the supreme penalty for murder in Utah. We have had almost a ten-year hiatus in the infliction of capital punishment. To deter a certain course of action, a threat must be perceived as real and not imaginary or illusory. During the period in which the death penalty constituted no *real* threat in the United States, the number of murders almost doubled, from roughly 10,000 to 20,000 a year.

This is not hard evidence that the threat of death, when perceived as a real threat, deterred murderers; but common sense sup-

121

"This is just a survey. If New York had the death penalty, would you consider another career?"

ports the inference that if, as the threat of the death penalty decreases, the rate of murders increases, then the corollary might well be true: if the threat had increased, the homicide rate might well have decreased.

The phenomenon of increased murder rates once the death penalty is removed is not unique to the United States. Canada abandoned hanging in 1967, and the number of murders climbed from 281 in that year to 426 in 1971, to 539 in 1974. The murder *rate* in Canada increased from 1.5 per 100,000 population in 1966 to 2.3 in 1971. England and Wales had 177 murders in 1971, the highest number since the death penalty was abolished in 1965.

On a nonscientific basis, we learn two things from these figures: first, murder goes up when the supreme penalty is removed, which may be too simple for the statisticians but may also account for the 23-percent increase in public favor for the death penalty in the past ten years. The average citizen tends to connect cause and effect as *he* perceives them, rather than as the behavioral scientists choose to explain them to him. Second, the abolitionists did not, with all their efforts to spare human life, create a climate of good will and gratitude among potential murderers. The sanctity of everyone's life but the killers' seems to have taken a precipitate nosedive.

Crimes of Passion

Another generalization. It has always been an article of faith among the abolitionists that many murders are committed by irrational people, in the heat of passion. Even if we had returned to the most *drastic* forms of capital execution—say, drawing and quartering in public—it would not deter *these* killings.

This argument is quite persuasive, but it begs the question. Capital punishment cannot and never will be able to deter *all* murderers. But this does not mean for a moment that it won't deter *any* murderers. When the criminal, particularly the murderer who *premeditates* his crime (the same murderer against whom most of the state capital murder statutes have been drawn) has an opportunity to weigh cost versus gain, cause and effect, he may well think twice if he knows that he will, in all likelihood, be put to death for his actions.

This reasoning was sufficient to satisfy the United States Supreme Court in *Gregg v. Georgia*. Justice Stewart held that:

> Although some of the studies suggest that the death penalty may not function as a significantly greater deterrent than lesser penalties, there is no convincing empirical evidence either supporting or refuting this view.
>
> We may nevertheless assume safely that there are murderers, such as those who act in passion, for whom the threat of death has little or no deterrent effect. But for many others, the death penalty undoubtedly is a significant deterrent. There are carefully contemplated murders, such as murder for hire, where the possible penalty of death may well enter the cold calculus that precedes the decision to act.

If we really don't know whether capital punishment deters, whose side are we to err on—the potential victims or the convicted murderers?

The question has been stated most lucidly by Professor van den Haag:

> If we do not know whether the death penalty will deter others, we are confronted with two uncertainties. If we impose the death penalty, and achieve no deterrent effect thereby, the life of a convicted murderer has been expended in vain (from a deterrent

viewpoint). There is a net loss. If we impose the death sentence and thereby deter some future murderers, we spared the lives of some future victims (the prospective murderers gain, too; they are spared punishment because they were deterred). In this case, the death penalty has led to a net gain, unless the life of a convicted murderer is valued more highly than that of the unknown victim, or victims (and the non-imprisonment of the deterred non-murderer).

The calculation can be turned around, of course. The absence of the death penalty may harm no one and therefore produce a gain—the life of the convicted murderer. Or it may kill future victims of murderers who could have been deterred, and thus produce a loss—their life.

To be sure, we must risk something certain—the death (or life) of the convicted man, for something uncertain—the death (or life) of the victims of murderers who may be deterred. This is in the nature of uncertainty—when we invest, or gamble, we risk the money we have for an uncertain gain. Many human actions, most commitments—including marriage and crime—share this characteristic with the deterrent purpose of any penalization, and with its rehabilitative purpose (and even with the protective). . . .

Ask the Criminals

The best way to find out if given criminals were indeed deterred from killing is to ask those criminals themselves. This has not been done very extensively, given the natural reluctance of the average perpetrator of violent crime to discuss his activities with the police, but some information from California is instructive. Certain felons

---

Everyone Fears Death

There is not one normal human being on the face of the earth who does not fear death. I do not believe this can be gainsaid. One is therefore led to the conclusion, probably oversimplistic, that death must be a deterrent. No one is going to attempt to cross the tracks at a subway station if he sees a train is coming. No one is going to open the door of an aircraft flying at 30,000 feet if he believes that, by so doing, he is bound to fall out. . . .It seems to me there are a large number of murders committed by persons who. . .are normal but for the commission of the crime of murder on their part. To them I say the death penalty is a deterrent.

Erik Nielsen, Commons abolition debate, May 3, 1976.

---

and would-be murderers *were* willing to talk, and it seems, if they can be believed, that the death penalty—when it was an actual, not a remote threat—deterred a lot of murders. Evidence to support this contention is found in a study conducted by the Los Angeles Police Department in 1970 and 1971 to measure the deterrent effect of the death penalty. Statements by persons arrested for crimes of violence were compiled. Those interviewed had been unarmed during the commission of their crimes, or had been armed but did not use their weapons, or had carried inoperative weapons. Ninety-nine persons gave a statement why they went unarmed or did not use their weapons. The results were classified as follows:

1. Deterred by fear of death penalty from carrying weapons or operative weapon, 50 (50%).
2. Unaffected by death penalty because it was no longer being enforced, 7 (7.07%).
3. Undeterred by death penalty, would kill whether it was enforced or not, 10 (10.1%).
4. Unaffected by death penalty because they would not carry weapon in any event, primarily out of fear of being injured themselves or of injuring someone else, 32 (32.3%).

Thus we see a five-to-one ratio of deterrence over nondeterrence as reported by individuals who were in the best position to make such a judgment: the criminals themselves. . . .

Criminals Fear the Death Penalty

Other sources give corroborating evidence that criminals fear the death penalty. Henry E. Peterson, then assistant attorney general for the criminal division of the United States Department of Justice, told the House of Representatives in 1972:

> It is not the Department's position that the death penalty deters in all cases. However, in some situations the evidence of the deterrent value of the penalty is very strong. . . .
>
> Newspapers carried the story of a prison break where an escaped convict released hostages at the State line, because, as he later told police when he was recaptured, he was afraid of the death penalty for kidnapping in the neighboring State. In the study I mentioned previously the American Bar Association reported instances where murderers have removed their victims from capital punishment States in order to avoid the threat of the death penalty. According to testimony given by the attorney general of Kansas and others before the Great Britain Royal Commission on Capital Punishment, these last-mentioned instances of murderers crossing State lines caused both Kansas and South Dakota to reintroduce the death penalty. It is the Department's position that if the threat of the death penalty deters the killing of innocent victims even to a limited extent, its retention is justified.

Carol S. Vance, the district attorney of Harris County (Houston), Texas tells us:

> The death penalty deterred an escape from a Texas prison. The inmate abducted a woman, stole her car, and headed west. When asked why he didn't kill this person who told police his direction of travel, [which] led to his capture, the inmate, already

under a life sentence, said he didn't want to ride "Old Sparky."
I have talked to robbers who said the only reason they didn't
kill the only eye witness was the threat of the electric chair. . . .

Start the Executions

We could resolve the question once and for all. We could start
executing murderers. Then, if we performed enough executions
to make the threat of death for willful premeditated murder an
actual threat again, and if the murder rate began to drop, we would
be able to determine (say, over ten years) that the threat of death,
when carried out, reduced the murder rate. *That* might give us
some empirical data about deterrence that we could get our teeth
into. Until this experiment is tried, we must concede that the deterrent arguments on either side are inconclusive. But I believe that
most people will agree with the rationale of Professor van den
Haag, stated above: given the uncertainty of deterrence, we should
resolve the question in favor of potential victims rather than convicted murderers.

Distinguishing Bias from Reason

The subject of capital punishment often generates great emotional response in people. When dealing with such a highly controversial subject, many will allow their feelings to dominate their powers of reason. Thus, one of the most important critical thinking skills is the ability to distinguish between opinions based upon emotion or bias and conclusions based upon a rational consideration of the facts.

Most of the following statements are taken from the viewpoints in this chapter. The rest are taken from other sources. Consider each statement carefully. *Mark R for any statement you believe is based on reason or a rational consideration of the facts. Mark B for any statement you believe is based on bias, prejudice, or emotion. Mark I for any statement you think is impossible to judge.*

If you are doing this activity as a member of a class or group, compare your answers with those of other class or group members. Be able to explain your answers. You may discover that others will come to different conclusions than you. Listening to the reasons others present for their answers may give you valuable insights in distinguishing between bias and reason.

If you are reading this book alone, ask others if they agree with your answers. You will find this interaction very valuable.

R = *a statement based upon reason*
B = *a statement based upon bias*
I = *a statement impossible to judge*

127

1. Robbery has increased sevenfold in two decades.

2. The volumes of materials available show that there is no consensus as to the cause of the rise in violent, predatory crime.

3. The broadening of suspects' rights by the Supreme Court has hampered the police to such an extent that they have been unable to do anything to reduce crime.

4. The legal extermination of human beings in any society generates a profound tendency among the citizens to accept killing as a solution to human problems.

5. There is a persistent finding that those states and counties which have abolished the death penalty have fewer capital crimes than do their neighbors which have retained capital punishment.

6. Only when committing murder is tantamount to committing suicide will the carnage abate.

7. The ivory towers are full of those far from the savagery of the streets; with knee-jerk certainty, they attack the death penalty believing it will brutalize the very society advocates say it will protect.

8. Killing human beings in order to solve social problems is deeply uncivilized.

9. We sentence people to death at the rate of about 250 a year.

10. People who would not dream of letting the government dictate what morning newspaper to read or what spouse to marry seem to have no problem with letting the government decide whom to kill.

11. If a crime is unpremeditated, it is unlikely that any threat of punishment would be a deterrent.

12. Any deterrent effect of the death penalty would be no more justification than the arguably even greater deterrent effect of prolonged torture or burning at the stake on the murder rate or the introduction of maiming as a penalty for burglary.

13. The costs of long-term incarceration turn out to be smaller than the costs of capital trials and extended appeals.

14. Capital punishment gives murderers the human responsibility of being accountable for their actions.

Periodical Bibliography

The following list of periodical articles deals with the subject matter of this chapter.

The Angolite	"Does the Death Penalty Deter?" July/August 1981. Available from Louisiana State Penitentiary, Angola, LA 70712.
Fred Barbash	"Two Old Men v. the Executioners," *The Washington Post National Weekly Edition*, December 19, 1983.
Philip Brasfield	"Charles Rumbaugh: A Study in Pain," *The Other Side*, January 1984.
James S. Granelli	"Justice Delayed," *American Bar Association Journal*, Vol. 70, January 1984.
Samuel R. Gross	"Speeding the Death Penalty Can Only Speed Injustice," *Los Angeles Times*, November 4, 1983.
Edward Koch	"Death & Justice," *New Republic*, April 15, 1985.
H.M. Metzenbaum	"Mistakes and the Death Penalty," *Harper's*, July 1984.
National Review	"Death Penalty Update," May 4, 1984.
David P. Phillips	"When Violence is Rewarded or Punished: The Impact of Mass Media Stories on Homicide," *Journal of Communication*, Summer 1984.
David P. Phillips	"Deterrent Effect of Capital Punishment: New Evidence on an Old Controversy," *American Journal of Sociology*, July 1980.
Marshall Shelley	"The Death Penalty: Two Sides of a Growing Issue," *Christianity Today*, March 2, 1984.
Robert Sherrill	"Death Row on Trial," *The New York Times Magazine*, November 13, 1983.
Faye A. Silas	"The Death Penalty," *American Bar Association Journal*, April 1985.
Ernest van den Haag	"New Arguments Against Capital Punishment," *National Review*, February 8, 1985.
Joy Williams	"The Angel of Death Row," *Esquire*, December 1985.
Franklin E. Zimring	"Idealizing the 'Angels' on Death Row," *Los Angeles Times*, February 24, 1983.

Should the Death Penalty Be Used for Political Crimes?

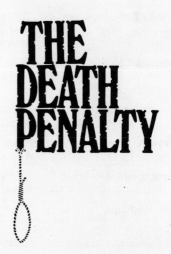

"The jury. . .had unanimously sentenced the two Italians to death, for they had both confessed to being anarchists and to rebelling against the present social order."

Sacco and Vanzetti Deserved the Death Penalty

Alvan T. Fuller and *The Literary Digest*

The 1927 trial and execution of Nicola Sacco and Bartolomeo Vanzetti in the state of Massachusetts is still debated. Scholars continue to uncover information that almost certainly proves their innocence for the murder with which they were initially charged. Their radical anarchist political views contributed greatly to their conviction and subsequent execution. The first part of the following viewpoint is taken from an interview with Alvan T. Fuller, governor of Massachusetts during the trial, who supported the death penalty for the Italian immigrants. The second part is excerpted from the periodical *The Literary Digest*.

As you read, consider the following questions:

1. Why was the execution of Sacco and Vanzetti opposed in Europe, according to the author?
2. What opportunity does the author believe that "radicals" found in the trial of Sacco and Vanzetti?
3. Why, according to a newspaper account, is the Sacco and Vanzetti case a justification for stricter immigration laws?

Living Age, "Governor Fuller in Berlin," November 1930. *The Literary Digest*, "What Does the Sacco-Vanzetti Case Teach?", September 3, 1927. The *Living Age* magazine ceased publication in 1941 and *The Literary Digest* ceased publication in 1938.

I

Former Governor Alvan T. Fuller of Massachusetts passed through Berlin last summer, where he was interviewed by a representative of the Weltbühne, *an influential radical weekly. The Sacco-Vanzetti case naturally figured in the conversation and Mr. Fuller took the opportunity to clear up certain misconceptions that he still finds lurking in the dark corners of the earth. On being asked whether attempts were still made against his life, he is said to have replied:—*

'Oh, you mean on account of Sacco and Vanzetti. Do you know that Europe has been much more upset about this affair than the United States? People in our country have not understood how so much excitement could be aroused about a couple of criminals. Both were convicted murderers and anarchists. Other countries make short work of such people but I did not uphold the death sentence against them until I had struggled for a long time with my conscience.'

'Yes, I read that in a Berlin paper under your picture.'

'You know, I had a hard time then. The jury, all of them unprejudiced, honorable men, had unanimously sentenced the two Italians to death, for they had both confessed to being anarchists and to rebelling against the present social order. They belonged to a brand of conspirators who attacked peaceful citizens with bombs and dynamite. They were for socialism and godlessness. The American people repudiate such frivolous ideas. In our country, everyone has complete freedom but he must not misuse it, and that is what these two men did.'

'Were you exposed to criticism in America?'

'Most people in America approved the verdict. It was clear to us that it was a purely American affair in which no foreigner was involved. The tendentious prejudice and general bitterness against the United States only damaged the two men. Perhaps without such pressure from outside another solution might have been possible.'

'A pardon?'

Proof of a Conspiracy

'Perhaps, but, in any case, the widespread support that Sacco and Vanzetti enjoyed abroad proved that there was a conspiracy against the security of the U.S.A. and that we should have to defend ourselves with every means at our disposal.'

'Do you perhaps know a certain Upton Sinclair?'

'Oh, that man is a crazy Bolshevik whom no one in America takes seriously. He was convicted in Boston for an immoral book. I believe it was entitled *Oil*. Such people have no practical significance among us Americans.'

'It is the same with us.'

'Moreover, some criminals later took revenge by attempting to

132

blow up the house of one of the jurymen. Then people recognized that Sacco and Vanzetti were criminals. But the whole affair has been forgotten long ago. No one in America thinks of it any more. There are so many criminals that we can't waste our time on these two.'

II

Since the original crime for which Sacco and Vanzetti were executed was a cruel one; since able counsel for the defense took advantage of every possible legal means of delaying execution; since Governor Fuller with the aid of President Lowell of Harvard, President Stratton of Massachusetts Institute of Technology, and Judge Robert Grant, after careful study endorsed the original verdict and the fairness of the trial, there are those who conclude that the case has come to its only possible end. For instance, the conservative Boston *Transcript* says emphatically:

> In view of the unchanging verdict of jury, courts, His Excellency the Governor, and the advisory committee, any other conclusion would have been sheer surrender to the forces of anarchy and disorder and an abject admission that trial by hysteria—which is nothing else than lynch law—had prevailed within the Commonwealth.
>
> This case has been the vehicle of as vicious propaganda as ever deluged a community. Radicals the world over saw here an opportunity to further what they call their cause. And the strange circumstance is that many well-meaning citizens either thought these foreign agitators were in earnest or were afraid of what they might do. The advice that they then gave was, on the one hand, the counsel of misguided sympathy; on the other, the counsel of fear. Massachusetts could accept neither.
>
> One thing more Massachusetts could not do and did not do. In the disposition of the case, she could not pay the slightest attention to European protests or the sentiments voiced by the journals and public men of distant lands. To have done so would have been, as Senator Borah expressed it, 'a national humiliation, a shameless, cowardly compromise of national courage.'
>
> Every citizen may rest assured that justice has been done.

Similarly, the Boston *Herald*, which months ago published a notable editorial declaring its doubt of the fairness of the trial, now declares its confident belief "that the agencies of law have performed their duties with fairness as well as justice." No less convinced, another Massachusetts paper, the Springfield *Union*, admitting that many never cease to doubt the justice of the verdict, remarks that: "if the element of doubt, however honest, in the minds of those, here and elsewhere, who lack the facts and the responsibility for justice, were to be set up as the supreme and final arbiter in criminal cases, there could never be a conviction and never be a prescribed penalty for crime." Perhaps never before, ventures the Portland (Me.) *Express* , "were two prisoners given so fair a chance for their lives."

The Washington *Post* is ashamed that many prominent American citizens "played into the hands of anarchy by credulity and sentimentality":

> They have believed the most preposterous lies and have been led into the false position of preferring to defeat justice rather than be accused of being unfair to accused men merely because they are anarchists. The abominable campaign of falsehood, perversion of testimony, intimidation, and bomb violence waged in behalf of these convicted assassins is an appalling revelation of what foreign cunning and money can do in delaying justice in this country.

The *Post* is convinced by this activity that "a thorough overhauling of nests of anarchists in this country should be made." The Sacco-Vanzetti case, agrees the Troy *Record*, "has brought home to Americans the danger of tolerating anarchy in modern society." Hence, we are told, "if the nation has learned this lesson from the Sacco-Vanzetti case, the deaths of these two men will have contributed valuably to the firmer solidarity of American institutions and to the greater safety of the nation." Good Americans are urged by the Pensacola *Journal* to "carry this fight into the Congress of the United States and insist that the Sacco-Vanzetti case form the basis of stricter immigration laws. There is no room in this country for foreigners who would come here to commit murder with the idea of escaping through protests registered by the world's radical and sentimental elements."

"Rightly or wrongly, the case of Sacco and Vanzetti goes down to history with the witch hunting in Salem."

Sacco and Vanzetti Did Not Deserve the Death Penalty

The Nation

Many people in the United States and in Europe were shocked and appalled at the execution of Nicola Sacco and Bartolomeo Vanzetti. Even though convicted primarily on circumstantial evidence, the Italian immigrants were executed promptly after their trial. In the following viewpoint, *The Nation*, a liberal periodical, calls the execution a rash injustice, declaring that it blackened the name of the United States.

As you read, consider the following questions:

1. What, according to *The Nation*, could Governor Fuller not see?
2. Why do the authors believe Sacco and Vanzetti should not have been executed?
3. What do the authors believe are the consequences of the execution?

The Nation, "Massachusetts the Murderer," August 31, 1927. Reprinted with permission, *The Nation* magazine, Nation Associates, Inc. © 1927.

Massachusetts has taken two lives with a vindictiveness and brutality unsurpassed in our history. It has blotted out the fishmonger and the cobbler whose names are now known around the world, men who in the minds of multitudes will take for the moment their places with the Carpenter. In the face of a world-wide protest of never-equalled dimensions, in the face of appeals from lawyers and judges of the highest standing, and from the heads of foreign governments—with complete contempt for the earnest pleas of the entire European press and some of the leading American daily newspapers that the guilt of the two men was not established beyond doubt—Governor Fuller and his council have sent Sacco and Vanzetti to their deaths. Henceforth the world over, when men wish to describe what is worst in any judicial system, they will declare that it is akin to Massachusetts justice; they will speak for years to come with horror of a State in which two men could be executed after seven years of monstrous torture, in the face of world-wide appeals for mercy; when the bar itself was divided as to the righteousness of the procedure; when the evidence was reviewed by only one judge and he was condemned for grave impropriety of conduct in connection with the case. Massachusetts, said Daniel Webster, "there she is." There she is today, a target for the opprobrium of mankind. Her constituted authorities have used their constitutional powers as cold-bloodedly as ever a Roman centurion had his legal way. . . .

"They Know Not What They Do"

Perhaps the greatest tragedy of all [is] that the men responsible have taken this course believing in their righteousness, their justice, yet utterly unable to see that the case of the accused had long since transcended the individuals concerned and become part of the lives and causes of great classes of our citizens. They, too, require forgiveness. "They know not what they do." They have had their eyes upon the Mosaic Law. No doubt Governor Fuller could not see a single just reason why he should commute or abate the sentence. "The Governor means well," wrote to *The Nation* last week one of the noblest persons connected with the cause of these men, who has sacrificed health and means to save the good name of the State of Massachusetts. "The trouble is," the writer added, *"he cannot see."* There lies the crux of the whole matter. He could not see that there are times when mercy is greater than justice and exalts justice. He could not feel the horror of this execution. He could not see that a wise statesman does not use to the fullest extent the power that is his when by staying the hand of the state he can soothe great masses of the public with an opportunity further to unwind the tangled skeins of evidence, so differently interpreted by those who have come into the case. He could not see that commutation would make possible the doing

136

of complete justice should later facts demand. So Massachusetts has legally murdered the fishmonger and the cobbler, vindictively and brutally, for all the righteousness of its Governor who cannot see. . . .

Political Views Influenced the Jury

The prosecution improperly capitalized the economic and political views of the defendants in an effort to prejudice the jury because of these views and to becloud the single issue of guilt or innocence of murder. There seems to be no idea that there could be no improper use of these views by the prosecution because the defendants themselves first introduced the subject. The point is very simple to a trial lawyer, and it is strange that there should be so much confusion about it.

When the defendants were arrested, they made certain false statements. The prosecution proved that the statements made by the defendants, when arrested, were false. If they had made no explanation of these false statements, they would have been in serious danger of conviction because false statements unexplained would have been taken as evidence of guilt of *murder*. The defendants, therefore, explained their false statements and their reasons for making them by testifying concerning their political and economic views and their fear of getting into trouble *because of their radical views*. Proper cross-examination by the prosecution would have been limited to an attempt to prove that the defendants were *not* "radicals"; were *not* "anarchists." Appropriate questions along this line would be, "Sacco, do you not know that you were election district captain for such and such district for so many years? Do you not know perfectly well that you served in the army during the War? Do you not know that you never attended a communist meeting in your life?"

Instead of which, it appears that the district attorney emphasized and capitalized and "rubbed in" the economic and political views of the defendants. He did not seek to show that their views and their fears were different from what they claimed them to be.

Emory R. Buckner, *The New Republic*, October 12, 1927.

It avails not to say that errors occur in the administration of justice in every land. This case has gone home to people because they are tortured with doubts about the justice of the sentence of two humble men with whom they have had no personal contact whatever, whose political views they in no wise share; because the human heart is not yet so corroded that it can read of the extinction of these two men without a shock to the very roots of its belief in justice and humanity. Perhaps it was precisely for the purpose of creating this sense of moral outrage in multitudes that

Alvan T. Fuller occupies the Governorship of Massachusetts. Perhaps fate intended that to millions should be brought home the utter folly of capital punishment, if only because of the terrible finality of it in a case in which new evidence has repeatedly appeared during these seven long years. Tomorrow the other three men charged with the killing who were never traced or identified may turn up; the stolen money not one cent of which was ever connected with Sacco and Vanzetti, may be discovered, and with it the solution of the crime. What then? Where then would be the Thayers and the Fullers? Convicted murderers in their turn. Who knows? . . .

Proof of Guilt Disputed

The point we make is that Governor Fuller has failed utterly to satisfy editors, lawyers, doctors, college presidents and professors, judges, and men of high standing everywhere, that the case was clear, the guilt beyond dispute. When a State takes the irrevocable step under conditions like these it is idle to talk of a deterrent. It is the State that has harmed itself, that has dealt a blow to law and order. It has roused a dreadful doubt which will never be dissipated, unless by the discovery of new evidence on one side or the other, during the lifetime of multitudes now living. Rightly or wrongly, the case of Sacco and Vanzetti goes down to history with the witch hunting in Salem and, in modern times, with the execution of the anarchists in Chicago in 1886. . . .

Whatever else may be said of Sacco and Vanzetti there can be no doubt that the souls of these two men grew and broadened and gained in knowledge and strength while they were behind the bars. When men face death many things are made clear to them; many scales drop from their eyes. We defy anyone to read Vanzetti's address to the court or Sacco's farewell to his son, and say that these were written by bloodstained hands. . . .

And these men the world is asked to believe were cowardly assassins and robbers, these men who led blameless lives until they are said to have appeared with three confederates—never traced—in a Buick car—never traced—to steal $16,000—never traced—in what police officials declared to be the manner of professional criminals.

They Have Made Their Mark

No, they may swallow this who will. To it we cannot bring our minds or our consciences. But innocent or guilty these men made their mark. Their bearing in the face of death, their shining courage, their resignation, the range of their spirits—these are deathless things, and somehow or other the memory of them goes on in the hearts of men. No one can say what it all means or foretell where this case will end. But this is clear: This legal murder in Boston will profoundly and adversely affect the international relations of the United States, and its moral standing throughout the world for at least a decade to come. Massachusetts has triumphantly killed an Italian fishmonger and an Italian cobbler, but she has blackened the name of the United States across all the seas.

"The Rosenbergs were mortal enemies, not merely of the United States, but of the entire human race."

The Death Penalty for the Rosenbergs Was Justified

America

Julius and Ethel Rosenberg were tried and convicted in March 1951 of transferring secret information about the atomic bomb to Russia. They were sentenced to death. Despite two years of delays and appeals, they were executed on June 19, 1953. The following viewpoint is taken from a 1953 issue of *America* magazine. The author argues that the Rosenbergs deserved to die for the actions which he believes put all of humanity in jeopardy.

As you read, consider the following questions:

1. What does the author think about the extensive legal arguments in the Rosenbergs' case?
2. How does the author think that the atomic age has changed espionage?
3. Why does the author think the United States was forced to "take the extreme measure"?

America, "Atomic-Age Executions," July 4, 1953. Reprinted with permission of America Press, Inc. 106 West 56th Street, New York, NY 10019. © All rights reserved.

The deaths of atomic spies Julius and Ethel Rosenberg in the electric chair at Sing Sing shortly after 8 P.M. on Friday, June 19, 1953 symbolized the age of atomic stakes into which the lives of nations have been catapulted. President Eisenhower, finally rejecting their pleas for clemency, observed:

> I can only say that, by immeasurably increasing the chances of atomic war, the Rosenbergs may have condemned to death tens of millions of innocent people all over the world.

Their crime, in sober truth, must be measured by a new calculus: the megadeath, or death of a million human beings. The Rosenbergs enabled Russia, by a mere silent threat of atomic warfare, to stand up to the free world pending what may be an atomic showdown of unimaginable carnage and devastation.

The Rosenbergs were mortal enemies, not merely of the United States, but of the entire human race. They were willing slaves of a conspiracy against humanity—unrepentant to the very end. The will to execute them was an affirmation by America, as the voice of humanity, of its will to survive. Only because they brazenly defied that will by refusing to name their accomplices did the Rosenbergs die. They died because such conspirators against humanity must either die or relent if humanity is to live.

End of Soft Treatment

There is hope that Federal Judge Irving Kaufman's sentencing of Julius and Ethel Rosenberg to die for stealing atomic secrets for transmission to Russia marks the end of our soft treatment of those who are disloyal. We can no longer afford the foolish indulgence of being soft with traitors. Judge Kaufman is to be congratulated for making that plain. Let other traitors be warned.

Editorial, *Constitution*, April 6, 1951.

The United States, forced to take the extreme measure of self-defense against which our humane feelings recoil, nevertheless afforded its traitors every conceivable legal recourse. It required great moral courage for Justice Douglas, convinced that a "substantial" legal question of the propriety of the death sentence under our law had been presented to him, to grant a stay at the eleventh hour. The ruling of the court against him, approved by a 6-3 vote, Justice Jackson's opinion defending the majority judgment and Mr. Douglas' opinion in dissent are noble monuments to the extreme care, amounting almost to scrupulosity, of American jurisprudence that no person, however guilty, however heinous his crime, shall die but by "due process of law." No American judge doubted the Rosenbergs' guilt.

Had the Rosenbergs hearts of flesh, they would have wept at

141

this concern. The very day they died our press reported the frightful story that tyrants to whom the spies had transferred their despicable loyalties had just sentenced to death and shot Willi Goettling, a poor, unemployed West Berlin painter, against whom, as an alleged instigator of riots, they bothered to publish no incriminating proof.

What are we to think of the handful of Congressmen who indulged their malice long enough to suggest the impeachment of Justice Douglas, just because his legal learning and moral scruples clashed with their "patriotic" passions? They knew not what they did. God grant that our courts may never be debauched into tools of political vengeance. That is part of our prayer on Independence Day, 1953.

"There is no precedent for a death penalty in a case like this. . . . Giving information to an ally. . .is not so serious as giving information to the enemy and. . .the penalty ought to be less."

The Death Penalty for the Rosenbergs Was Not Justified

Arthur Garfield Hays

This article was written in November 1952, just seven months before the Rosenbergs were executed. The author, who at the time was a general counsel for the American Civil Liberties Union, voices feelings that were held worldwide during the trial and even after the execution. While Mr. Hays does not argue for the Rosenbergs' innocence, he is convinced that this "horrible killing by the state" is not merited and that the Rosenbergs would best be punished in a more humane way.

As you read, consider the following questions:

1. How does the author think the Rosenbergs' case compares to other espionage cases of the time?
2. What differences does the author see between Russia as our ally and Russia as our enemy? How does this affect the decision in the Rosenbergs' trial?
3. What ramifications does this case suggest to the author?

Arthur Garfield Hays, "The Rosenberg Case," *The Nation*, November 8, 1952. Reprinted with permission, *The Nation* magazine, Nation Associates, Inc. © 1952.

Julius and Ethel Rosenberg are held in Sing Sing prison awaiting execution. They were given the death penalty by Judge Irving R. Kaufman, having been found guilty of violating the Espionage Act by supplying secret information to Russia. Said the sentencing judge: "I consider your crime worse than murder."

The judgment was affirmed by the United States Court of Appeals. Certiorari was denied by the United States Supreme Court. At this writing a rehearing is under consideration by that court.

Why the uneasiness about this case? Is it due to leftist propaganda? What support, if any, is there for the claim that these people are innocent, or that they did not have a fair trial?

It is true that they were convicted on the testimony of co-conspirators and confessed spies. It is charged that the testimony of Greenglass and his wife, the chief witnesses against the Rosenbergs, was induced by an agreement with the prosecutor that Ruth Greenglass would not be prosecuted and that David Greenglass would receive a relatively light sentence.

The Charges

Julius and Ethel Rosenberg, together with David Greenglass, Anatoli Yakolev, and Morton Sobell, were charged with conspiracy to violate the Espionage Act by communicating secret information to Russia between 1944 and 1950, with intent and reason to believe that the information was to be used to the advantage of Russia. Harry Gold, who had pleaded guilty in another court, and Ruth Greenglass were named in the indictment as co-conspirators, not as defendants. David Greenglass, a brother of Ethel Rosenberg, was stationed as a soldier at the Los Alamos Atomic Experimental Station. He testified that he conveyed information and sketches to the Rosenbergs and their emissaries which, it was charged, they turned over to Russia. Harry Gold had, at the command of Yakolev, met with Klaus Fuchs, the British scientist and Russian spy working at Los Alamos. Greenglass testified that Julius Rosenberg admitted to him that he transmitted information to Russia on micro-film equipment and that he received rewards from the Russians in money and gifts. Rosenberg also, according to Greenglass, was associated in some way with Jacob Golos, his go-between having been Elizabeth Bentley. After Fuchs was arrested, the evidence showed that Rosenberg gave Greenglass some $5,000 which Greenglass claimed was to enable him to leave the country. Rosenberg himself and his wife had passport photographs taken, apparently contemplating a getaway. The facts are complicated, but if Greenglass is to be believed they fit into a picture like pieces of a jigsaw puzzle, implicating all the defendants in the conspiracy to transmit information to Russia.

Russia was our ally in 1944, but under the statute a crime exists if secret information is turned over to a foreign government with reason to believe that the information may be of advantage to the recipient. The charge was not treason. The defendants were not indicted or tried for giving aid to an enemy. In a treason trial there would have been certain constitutional safeguards. Thus, the defendants argue that the crime of which they were accused was of the same kind of treason but of a lesser degree, and that they were at least entitled to the constitutional protections which would have been required in a treason trial. Further, the argument runs that traditionally and by statute the courts have been authorized to impose the death penalty for treason, and that to authorize such a sentence for a similar but less grave offense is to permit cruel and unusual punishment in violation of the Constitution. It was argued that the political views of the defendants, the fact that they were Communists, naturally prejudiced the jury against them, and that the question of whether or not they were Communists should have played no part in the trial. The court held that this evidence was relevant. Said Judge Frank of the United States Court of Appeals:

> An American's devotion to another country's welfare cannot of course constitute proof that he has spied for that other country. But the jurors may reasonably infer that he is more likely to spy for it than other Americans not similarly devoted.

It is alleged that the concept of treason was emphasized during the trial, although that was not the crime charged. The answer is that the term "treason" was used in a general, not in a technical sense.

Guilt Irrelevant

What remain important as the day of execution approaches are deeper considerations of humanity and mercy and an honest weighing of the Rosenbergs' offense against the irreparable punishment they face. It is not necessary to challenge their guilt; it is essential to ask whether the crime they committed, in the circumstances under which they committed it, justifies death. . . .

It would be absurd to minimize the crime of which they were convicted. Whether or not it was "worse than murder," as Judge Kaufman declared, it was bad enough. But it was not treason, and it was not spying in behalf of an enemy country—however hard it is to keep that in mind in the atmosphere of cold war.

The Nation, January 10, 1953.

The jury has spoken. The Appellate Court has spoken; the opinion of Judge Frank began, "Since two of the defendants must be put to death if the judgment stands, it goes without saying that we have scrutinized the record with extraordinary care."

In view of all this, why the fuss about the Rosenbergs? The

answer lies in the penalty, the sentence of death. Julius and Ethel Rosenberg are lodged in Sing Sing awaiting execution. As the trial court said, it is hard to conceive of a crime which, as events have transpired, could have more vicious consequences. Yet we cannot forget that Klaus Fuchs, the scientist and chief conspirator in this whole business, was tried in England and sentenced to only fourteen years in jail, and that in the Canadian spy trials the sentences were relatively light. We may try, but we cannot forget the two young Rosenberg children.

So far as I know, there is no precedent for a death penalty in a case like this. We cannot help feeling that giving information to an ally (we must bear in mind, however, that the Rosenbergs continued to give information when Russia was no longer an ally and was in a sense an enemy) is not so serious as giving information to the enemy and that if this is a lesser crime the penalty ought to be less. These considerations apparently moved Circuit Judge Frank, who felt constrained to hold that the appellate court had no power to reduce the sentence. Judge Frank said:

> In support of that contention [that the penalty should be reduced] they assert the following: that they did not act from venal or pecuniary motives; except for this conviction, their records as citizens and parents are unblemished; at the most, out of idealistic motives they gave secret information to Soviet Russia when it was our wartime ally; for this breach they are sentenced to die, while those who, according to the government, were their confederates, at least equally implicated in wartime espionage—Harry Gold, Emil Fuchs, Elizabeth Bentley, and the Greenglasses—get off with far lighter sentences or go free altogether. Finally, they argue, the death sentence is unprecedented in a case like this: No civil court has ever imposed this penalty in an espionage case, and it has been imposed by such a court in two treason cases only.

There is a suggestion in connection with the death penalty that the Supreme Court might "well think it desirable to review that aspect of our decision in the case."

The Death Penalty

It is the damnable death penalty that causes the uneasiness. To avoid this horrible killing by the state, argument is made that the trial was unfair, and some people, mostly leftists I take it, are claiming that the Rosenbergs are innocent. If this judgment is carried through, we shall make martyrs of the Rosenbergs, perhaps not to many people in the United States, but to millions in other parts of the world. You can imagine what would be our own emotional response if two Russians were sentenced to death for supplying information to us while we were allied with Russia. Somehow, I cannot help feeling that the British treatment of Fuchs shows a higher degree of civilization than the sentence in this case.

"The sale of US defense secrets for financial gain. . .can be controlled only when the perception of retribution is high and the nature of the promised retribution is severe."

The Walkers' Treason Merited the Death Penalty

Elmo Zumwalt and Worth Bagley

In mid-1985, John A. Walker Jr., a former military officer, was arrested and charged with heading a family-based spy ring which sold secret information to the Soviets. The case aroused great alarm and focused public debate on the question of appropriate punishment for treason. The authors of the following viewpoint, Elmo Zumwalt and Worth Bagley, are among the many who believe that the death penalty is the only appropriate punishment for such a crime. Mr. Zumwalt and Mr. Bagley, both retired navy admirals and syndicated columnists, wrote this viewpoint in response to the conviction of John Walker. They express their belief that Mr. Walker's crime deserved a death sentence.

As you read, consider the following questions:

1. What are the three reasons the authors cite for people becoming involved in espionage?
2. What do the authors find particularly repulsive about the Walkers' crimes?
3. Do the authors believe the death penalty would be a deterrent to future spies?

Elmo Zumwalt and Worth Bagley, "Tougher Penalties for Selling Secrets," *The Washington Times*, August 21, 1985. © 1985, Los Angeles Times Syndicate. Reprinted with permission.

On August 9, 1985 the first of what will be several trials in the Walker spy ring case came to an end as retired Lt. Cmdr. Arthur J. Walker was found guilty of espionage on all seven counts with which he had been charged. . . .

Since the arrest of John Walker on May 20 and the subsequent arrests of his alleged co-conspirators, various measures have been proposed to curb such espionage activity in the future. Some measures, such as the Department of Defense decision to reduce the number of authorized clearances, seek to focus on the problem by reducing the size of the population that has actual access to classified material. Other measures, such as congressional support of the death penalty for those convicted of peacetime espionage by military courts, seek to focus on penalties. (Under existing laws at the time of the alleged Walker espionage activity, the most severe penalty that can be imposed on any of the alleged conspirators is life imprisonment.)

While there is almost unanimous agreement that the former measures represent an important first step in dealing with the problem, there has been much discussion and disagreement about the latter measures. The familiar argument is made once again—just as it has been in recent years in connection with efforts to reinstitute capital punishment—that the death penalty does not serve as a deterrent to objectionable behavior.

Tolerance Related to Motives

There are three main reasons why one engages in espionage: (1) loyalty to another country or ideal, (2) revenge against the victim state, and (3) financial gain. Interestingly, citizens of Communist bloc nations who spy against their country appear, for the most part, to be motivated by a commitment to ideals different from those of their own country, while their Free World counterparts appear to be motivated more by greed.

But it is clear that our society's tolerance of a specific act of espionage varies directly with the reason why the act in question was originally undertaken. For example, more seem willing to accept the spy who acts out of loyalty to his country or out of a sense of commitment to other ideals. A smaller number seem willing to accept the spy whose better judgment is, perhaps, temporarily impaired by blind emotion, such as revenge.

Motivated by Greed

But our society contains very few who are willing to tolerate the spy whose motivation stems primarily from financial gain. The majority of the people we have interviewed believe it is the spy who puts his personal gain above the security of his country that should be held most accountable for his actions.

In response to this majority position, legislation is before Congress that seeks the public execution, by firing squad, of anyone convicted of espionage for financial gain. We fully support such a measure. The spy motivated by financial gain fully understands the nature of his act and why he has undertaken to perform it; he has weighed both the risks and the rewards, and has opted in favor of self-gratification over the welfare and security of his countrymen.

Bill Garner for *The Washington Times.* Reprinted with permission.

The claim that imposing the death penalty for such an act of espionage will not serve as a deterrent, we feel, lacks merit. When espionage is committed for financial gain, it is committed by a rational individual who knows he has chosen between right and wrong. In opting to violate the espionage laws, he has perceived that the risks of getting caught are low, the rewards are high, and the retribution society will exact should the act be discovered is not great.

This perception has been fostered by a country which, ever since the execution of Julius and Ethel Rosenberg in June 1953, has been suprisingly tolerant toward those who have sold its defense secrets. That tolerance has continued—inexcusably, we believe—despite the fact that American lives, in some instances, have subsequently been lost due to the disclosure of classified information. (Such was the case of Joseph G. Helmich, who was convicted in 1980 of supplying code secrets to the Soviets in the 1960s, enabling them to monitor U.S. military operations in Vietnam and contributing to the loss of many American lives there.)

The sale of U.S. defense secrets for financial gain—like most other kinds of behavior—can be controlled only when the perception of retribution is high and the nature of that promised retribution is severe. Such an approach has been effective in holding down the number of capital crimes committed in many Middle East countries, where the penalty imposed for those crimes includes death or mutilation.

For more than two centuries Americans have died on battlefields the world over to preserve our freedom and security. In battles yet to be fought, it is probable that many American lives may be lost due to classified information that someone has sold to our enemies.

Is it unfair to demand, in exchange, the life of one who has endangered our freedom and security or has increased the risk to our fighting men on the battlefield by selling this country's defense secrets to an unfriendly nation? We believe not.

"As a deterrent to espionage [the death penalty] is worthless."

The Death Penalty for the Walkers Would Have Been Senseless

Don Edwards and Henry Schwarzschild

The following viewpoint is excerpted from two articles written before the sentencing of John Walker and his cohorts, all of whom ultimately received prison sentences. Part I is by Don Edwards, the Democratic representative from California, and chairman of the House Judiciary Subcommittee on Civil and Constitutional Rights. Part II is an interview with Henry Schwarzschild, the director of the American Civil Liberties Union's Capital Punishment Project. The authors argue that the death penalty for spies like the Walkers would accomplish nothing. Other governmental measures such as declassifying more information and better background checks on employees would be more effective in cutting down on spying.

As you read, consider the following questions:

1. What does Mr. Edwards believe would happen to the Walkers, even if they had received the death penalty?
2. Does Mr. Schwarzschild believe that spies endanger American national security? Why or why not?
3. Does Mr. Schwarzschild believe the death penalty would deter those who spy for financial gain?

I

Revelations about the scope and duration of the alleged Walker spy ring make it clear that our system for protecting vital secrets needs a major overhaul. It is thus distressing to see how quickly some officials have seized upon the case to resurrect a long-discredited idea: the death penalty. . . .

As a deterrent to murder, the death penalty is of dubious value. As a deterrent to espionage, it is worthless.

First, the Walker ring, if convicted, will never face the electric chair since any death statute enacted now would not apply to its members. Second, future spies would rarely be executed. Many captured spies are never tried because we hope to convert them into double agents or because the damage to national security would be aggravated by disclosure of further secrets. When we do convict spies, we tend to trade them for agents of our own. As Henry Schwarzschild of the American Civil Liberties Union has pointed out, an executed spy is no bargaining chip. Third, the theoretical prospect of the death penalty is not likely to have much effect on the cold-blooded spy. Traitors for hire, like killers for hire, do not expect to be caught. For them, the difference between life imprisonment and a death sentence is meaningless. . . .

A Get-Tough Approach

The death penalty . . . exemplifies a get-tough approach that makes us feel good but accomplishes little. At hand are less dramatic, more effective proposals.

There seems to be a developing consensus that one feature of our security system above all others has contributed to the crisis: too many people have access to classified material. Before we can cut down on the number of security clearances, we have to address a second feature: excessive classification. When everything is classified, everyone must have a clearance, even to do the most ordinary work. If we classify only what is valuable to the Kremlin, we could focus our resources on safe-guarding that information.

The Administration, which shares blame for overclassifying information, recognizes that in its efforts to protect everything it has hampered its ability to protect anything. As Attorney General Edwin Meese 3d has said: "A lot of things which shouldn't be classified are, and therefore there is a kind of ho-hum attitude toward the protection of national security information."

If the Reagan Administration cuts back on the amount of information classified and the number of people with clearances, we can then address a third problem: the sizable backlog in reclearance checks. Follow-up investigations are supposed to be made every five years for access to top secret data, but recertifications are running 10 years behind. We should regularly recheck employees and cancel the clearances of those who no longer need them. Finally, we should redouble efforts against the real culprits—the thousands of KGB and Eastern bloc agents operating in this country. They should be the focus of our attention, not the millions of Americans who serve in the military and defense-related industries.

In our eagerness to do something in response to the Walker allegations, let us at least take the time to do something effective.

II

Q. *Mr. Schwarzschild, why do you oppose legislation to authorize the death penalty for convicted spies in peacetime?*

A. The American Civil Liberties Union and I myself oppose the death penalty for any crime as uncivilized, brutalizing and useless. An execution is a premeditated act of homicide under law. We oppose its use even against murderers and certainly in cases of peacetime espionage, where there is no taking of human life.

Most Spies Are Irrational

It is perfectly true that capital punishment would act as a deterrent if those about to engage in espionage were calculating rationally the risks involved. But most spies are not very rational, let alone farsighted, and in any case they are convinced that *they* will never get caught.

Walter Laqueur, *The New Republic*, July 29, 1985.

The insistence by members of the Reagan administration and others that espionage ought to be a capital offense even in peacetime reflects a tendency to put our society on a permanent war footing, to create a garrison state and to make national-security considerations preeminent, as though we were constantly at war. That is very ominous.

Q. *We execute murderers. Doesn't someone who threatens the survival of a whole nation in the nuclear age deserve equally severe punishment?*

A. It's extremely doubtful that acts of espionage have threatened the life of our society. Take the Rosenbergs. I happen to believe they were guilty as charged, but the proposition that national security required their execution because they threatened the life of this nation turned out to be baseless and founded on hysteria.

And even if a spy does constitute a threat of that magnitude, we can secure ourselves against him by putting him in jail and thus incapacitating him from causing further damage. We do not, however, have the right to kill.

Q. *Doesn't the large number of recent espionage cases suggest that people are not deterred by the threat of jail?*

A. Spies are of two kinds: Rational or irrational. The first kind will be deterred as much by the prospect of 40 years in a federal penitentiary as by worries about the death penalty. The second kind won't be deterred by anything.

Catch More Spies

Q. *Wouldn't the prospect of capital punishment stop some people who spy only for financial reward?*

A. For someone who spies for a $30,000 fee, the prospect of 40 years or more in jail would seem to be as much—or as little—of a deterrent as the death penalty. The best defense against spies is to catch more of them—not to punish them in a Draconian fashion.

Q. *Isn't imprisonment often ended prematurely by parole?*

A. Parole boards, like other agencies of justice, are human and therefore make occasional mistakes. That is all the more reason not to entrust judicial agencies with the decision as to whether someone is to live or die.

Q. *Can't traitors always hope to win their freedom in one of the periodic spy exchanges between the U.S. and the Soviet Union?*

A. Yes, but that applies as well to the spies we have in the Soviet Union and whom we want to get back through such exchanges. Spies we catch here will not make good bargaining chips if we execute them.

"An act of treason . . . might induce Soviet leaders to . . . carry out a preemptive strike and so provoke unlimited thermonuclear war."

The Damage Done by Spies Warrants the Death Penalty

Paul Johnson

Paul Johnson is a former editor of *The New Statesman* and the author of a book called *Modern Times*. In the following viewpoint, Mr. Johnson explains his belief that a citizen who spies for a totalitarian enemy is guilty of the worst crime imaginable and should be punished proportionately.

As you read, consider the following questions:

1. How does the author define an act of treason?
2. What does the author believe could happen to our society as a result of espionage activities?
3. How does the author reason that the death penalty fits the crime of espionage?

Paul Johnson, "Death to Spies—the Worst Criminals," *Los Angeles Times*, June 28, 1985. Reprinted by permission of the author.

For a citizen of a democracy under the rule of law to spy for an expansionist, totalitarian enemy falls into the most serious category of offenses that a human being is capable of committing.

Even within this category, however, there are degrees of atrocity. The offense is more grave if the guilty man or woman is a member of the armed forces or another government agency and thus is in breach of oath and trust. The worst case of all is where the offender's position in the state service gives access to information of the highest secrecy and importance, and where this is the subject of the treason.

Freedom in Jeopardy

We have in such a case a crime of unique depravity. It is worse than mass murder, for one has to assume—and the offender, in committing it, made the assumption—that the information conveyed could, in the event of war, lead to the deaths of hundreds—perhaps thousands, perhaps even millions—of compatriots, a slaughter far beyond the capacity of a single assassin.

In the peculiar circumstances of the Cold War the crime acquires an added degree of wickedness. It is well known that the United States forms the only real military barrier to Soviet expansion, and that if this barrier were removed, free institutions and people everywhere would be in jeopardy. It is also well known that the United States maintains this barrier largely by its technological superiority in certain arcane areas of military science.

An act of treason that substantially, or perhaps even decisively, reduces this margin of superiority would produce calamitous consequences. It might induce Soviet leaders to make a fatal miscalculation about their own relative power, to prepare and carry out a preemptive strike and so provoke unlimited thermonuclear war. In the hundreds of millions of deaths that would follow, the original act of espionage would plainly be a prime causative factor.

Crime Against Humanity

Alternatively, the information conveyed might be of so decisive a nature as to give the Soviets an undeniable military advantage, and force the United States into a posture of appeasement or surrender. That would leave the Soviet Union, one of the most ruthless and destructive tyrannies that the world has ever known, alone on the stage, able to impose its will by the threat or use of force everywhere. No such global despotism has ever been established before in the whole of history. It would be a durable despotism, too, for who or what would have the power to overthrow it?

The original act of treason, then, would be a crime not just against the state, not just against all its citizens, imperiling their lives or their liberties or both. It would be a crime against a huge portion of humanity, against all those who choose to live in societies based on consent and the process of law. Indeed, it would be a crime against posterity, too, for its consequences might well commit unborn generations to live their lives in servitude.

Deter Would-Be Spies

How can a crime of this magnitude be punished adequately? It seems to me that to deprive the convicted felon of his or her life is the only way a civilized society can respond both prudently and justly.

Prudently, for two reasons:

First, deterrence. The age of the ideological traitor is over; the age of the mercenary traitor has begun. For spies who convey secrets not from conviction but for money, who are motivated by a rational calculation of greed, the death penalty is an undoubted deterrent.

Jeopardizing Millions

Opinion polls show that in aggravated cases of murder, most Americans support capital punishment. What, then, should be the penalty for a traitor who jeopardizes the lives of thousands or even millions? In our dangerous world, passing security secrets to the Soviet Union could result in the death of millions. No punishment—even death—is adequate for such a crime.

It is often asserted that only God should determine when a man should die and that the state has no right to take a man's life. In fact, the state does have a right to ask a man to give up his life in defense of home and country. As we are indebted to the hundreds of thousands of Americans who have made this supreme sacrifice, so we are morally compelled to end the lives of traitors who imperil our freedom and security.

Ernest W. Lefever, "Give Spies the Death Penalty," *New York Times*, July 22, 1985.

The second utilitarian calculation is that the Soviet spymasters have repeatedly taken advantage of the West's unwillingness to execute spies. Some, like British master spy George Blake, they have actually sprung from jail. They have negotiated the release of others, sometimes by arresting Western citizens on trumped-up charges. There is thus no absolute guarantee that a spy sentenced to life imprisonment will serve it. It is a comfort to actual spies and an encouragement to would-be spies that, even in the worst possible circumstances, the most that they will face is prison, and that even there they are under the long, protective arm of the KGB.

But the most compelling argument in favor of the death penalty is the argument from justice. The function of punishment in the system of justice is not merely to deter, not merely to protect society, but to distinguish between the relative gravity of crimes by the relative severity of the penalty. Thousands of crimes (some quite minor) are punished by imprisonment, and those so punished serve their time together. For the state to deprive an offender of liberty is, to put it bluntly, of no great consequence. It happens in hundreds of cases every day.

On the other hand, for a civilized society to deprive one of its members of his life is an awesome thing. It is an act of great finality and calculated horror. It is, in a way, the most tremendous act of which a human society is capable, in which it comes closest to arrogating to itself the authority of the divine.

Precisely because it inspires awe and even horror, no other human act of justice is more likely to bring home to the public the peculiar atrocity of the crime to which it is the judicial response. To execute a criminal is to say, loudly and vividly: "This creature has done a thing so dreadful that we must inflict on him the supreme penalty in our power." Over the centuries, nearly all civilized societies have reserved mandatory execution for murder, rightly judging that murder must be isolated as the most atrocious of crimes, to be presented to the public mind as such by the uniqueness of the penalty.

Now we are confronted by a crime that, by its actual and potential effects, is worse than murder, embracing murder and indeed mass murder and much else besides—a crime on a scale that the human mind finds difficulty in comprehending. For such a crime, death is not the complete answer; there is none. But it is the only commensurate answer in our power.

"The contention of the military, foreign policy, and intelligence establishments that if disclosed their secrets could practically start a war with the Soviet Union is . . . utterly unconvincing."

The Damage Done by Spies Does Not Warrant the Death Penalty

David Kahn

Inspired by the public outcry about the treason trials of John A. Walker and his spy ring, David Kahn writes in the following viewpoint that the importance of spy cases such as this one is overblown. A *Newsday* editor and the author of two books, *The Codebreakers* and *Hilter's Spies*, Mr. Kahn points out that hysteria and media hype often magnify the damage done by spies in today's technological age. He therefore believes that espionage does not merit the death penalty.

As you read, consider the following questions:

1. Why does the author believe that complex technology protects us against spies?
2. What role does the author think the press plays in coloring our opinions of spies?

David Kahn, "High-Tech Secrets," *The Nation*, August 31, 1985. Reprinted with permission, *The Nation* magazine, Nation Associates, Inc. © 1985.

Government representatives and scare headlines portray the alleged spy ring of John A. Walker Jr. and his confederates as a knife to the heart of American national security. Neither the government nor the press knows in detail what information Walker and the others may have passed to the Soviet Union, but I believe the damage is not as great as the hysteria makes it seem.

Size and complexity protect modern military systems. A submarine, for example, has propulsion, sonar, radar and weapons subsystems, each with its own construction specifications, technical manuals and operating instructions. Although 129 classified documents were found in one bag seized by the F.B.I. and fifteen pounds of documents were found near the bunk of another suspect, these and the other material delivered over the years amount to a drop in the bucket compared with the tons of paper and billions of bytes needed to run the military today. Nor can an entire system—even an entire operation within that system—be understood from its components. Revealing the sensitivity of the sonobuoys used to track Soviet submarines would not disclose the pattern-recognition techniques used to discriminate between the sonar echoes returned by whales, schools of fish and submarines.

Obsolete Secrets

Beyond that, secrets become obsolete. Suppose that five years ago the spy ring gave the Russians documents showing the speed at which Soviet submarines are detectable by the United States. By now, advances in ocean acoustics, sensors, microprocessors and mathematics will almost certainly have lowered that figure.

There are also economic and political limitations on the usefulness of purloined information. Before the United States entered World War II, German spies stole the Norden bombsight, whispered to be the nation's biggest secret. But the Luftwaffe had installed its own bombsight, the Lothfe, and did not want to replace it with the Norden and retrain all the bombardiers. The effect of the great spy coup was almost nil. In the same way, the Soviet Union has produced a class of submarines, the Alfa, that is fast but noisy. The Russians chose speed over silence for their own reasons, and more detailed knowledge of American antisubmarine warfare probably wouldn't induce them to make fundamental chages.

Computer Safeguards

Moreover, the purported cryptographic loss is not as severe as some accounts suggest. Because one member of the alleged ring had been a cryptographic equipment repairman for the Navy, the press and Defense Department officials claim that he could have given the Russians details of U.S. cryptosystems. But the heart of today's cipher machines is probably a computer chip bonded in epoxy. Various safeguards make that chip almost impossible to steal. Furthermore, knowledge of the general cryptographic system, the part embodied in the chip, does not by itself enable a cryptanalyst to read a message. He or she also needs the specific keys that control the variables of that system. Today those keys may be stored in read-only memories and inserted automatically into the cipher machine; the human operator never knows what they are. Or a computerized key-management center may generate fresh keys and send them to the cipher machine, again without the operator's participation. And because keys usually change from message to message, even knowledge of both the general system and the keys for a message will allow cryptanalysts to read only that message.

An Alert

Defense Secretary Caspar Weinberger sent out an ominous signal when he called for the execution of those who pass military secrets to "hostile" powers in peacetime.

Such hysterical statements . . . that anyone convicted of spying "be shot" is part of administration efforts to create a "siege mentality" in the U.S., the kind of thinking that had some looking under their beds for Communists . . . during the McCarthy era.

What does Weinberger consider a military secret? When the U.S. invaded Grenada, the media was barred from reporting the events under the guise of defending national security. If a reporter had been able to get out information on the invasion, would he or she have been shot for doing so under Weinberger's proposal? During the Vietnam war, publication of the Pentagon papers exposed many of the lies behind the U.S. role. Would Weinberger have shot those who exposed the lies?

Daily World, June 26, 1985.

For that reason, a recent *New York Times* report that "the Soviet Union was able to make use of coding machines taken from the American spy ship Pueblo in 1968 to read coded traffic" is nonsense. At worst, a few messages to and from the Pueblo might have been read. Because of advances in semiconductor and computer technology, new cipher machines have certainly been introduced since 1968.

Death Penalty out of Proportion

The same news story stated that one member of the alleged ring "gave the Soviet Union years of access to the Navy's satellite communications network" by revealing the "secret" frequencies "over which communications were being broadcast from satellites." In fact, those frequencies have been published. For instance, FLEET-SATCOM Frequency Plan Alpha Channel 18 at 260.775 megahertz is one of the Navy's communications satellite downlinks. And anyone with a dish antenna almost anywhere in the hemisphere can hear the signals simply by scanning the frequency spectrum, just as a radio listener can tune across the dial, seeking rock music or a ball game.

Feeding the spying hype is the excessive secrecy in government. The basis for grading material "top secret" is that its loss would cause "exceptionally grave damage to the national security." The contention of the military, foreign policy and intelligence establishments that if disclosed their secrets could practically start a war with the Soviet Union is, to anyone who has ever read those banal documents, utterly unconvincing.

The Walker case hype has served some purposes. It has helped sell newspapers and magazines and raise television ratings. It has justified larger appropriations for the counterespionage agencies. It has perhaps made it easier to restore the death penalty for espionage in peacetime—a punishment that in this case at least is far out of proportion to the damage apparently done. But it has not served the truth. Sometimes spy rings are blown; this one was overblown.

The Death Penalty
and Treason:
Ranking Values

The authors of the viewpoints in this chapter debate the merits of imposing the death penalty for treasonous acts. It is clear that each of the authors holds some concerns to be of more importance than others. For example, one writer thinks that treason is a betrayal of all the people of a nation and therefore should be punished by death; another thinks that little actual harm is caused by many acts of treason and therefore the death penalty is inappropriate. This activity will allow you to think about your own values relating to the death penalty and treason.

Below is a list of situations, all of which might be interpreted as treasonous by someone. *Beside each situation, mark a D if you believe it describes a situation which should be punished by the death penalty. Mark a P if you believe it merits some form of punishment but not the death penalty. Leave it blank if you believe the situation should not be punished at all.*

_____   A student writes an article about how to build a neutron bomb; the materials he bases his article on are in his college library but they are not widely available to the public—or to foreign countries—until this paper is published.

_____   A young scientist is disillusioned with the defense policies of his country, thinking they will lead to a nuclear war. Believing the only way to prevent a world war is to equalize world power, he gives secret research information to his country's strongest competitor.

_____ A young woman in a highly sensitive government job is well-paid and ambitious. When approached by spies of an enemy country to sell top-secret information for large amounts of money, the woman does so, knowing the extra money could be put toward her life-long dream—a fire red Maserati.

_____ A group of eight friends work in a highly classified government department. Routinely, they chat about their work with two foreign friends who are part of their social group. Although it's not openly discussed, all of these people know that this information is given by the foreigners to their government.

_____ A gay man works in a high security research facility where homosexuality is considered a security risk and a reason for dismissal. A foreign agent has evidence of this man's homosexuality and threatens to expose him if he doesn't pass secret information to the agent. Knowing he will lose his job if he doesn't agree, he gives the agent all the information he asks for.

_____ A military man with top secret clearance sells unclassified documents to the Soviet Union for financial gain.

_____ A foreign spy manages to get access to top secret information which could be damaging to this country.

_____ A woman sincerely believes that her country's policies are harming its people and that her country's competitor has the right system for helping all the people. Believing that she cannot change the harmful system of her country in any other way, she sabotages her country by stealing secret information and giving it to the competing country, by undermining important projects she has access to, and by working with an underground group whose goal is to destroy her country's political system.

_____ A group of people who do not agree with its country's political policy form an organization which has the goal of overthrowing the government. They organize rallies and demonstrations to try to get other people to join with them in a revolution.

_____ A group of eight people is caught and convicted of selling secrets to a foreign power. The community is outraged, but the first two spies are let off on a technicality; the third one commits suicide; the next two are given ten-year prison sentences. The public seems to be demanding the death penalty for the last two spies.

_____ A group of people who do not agree with their country's political policies belong to a radical revolutionary organization. They believe that the only way to change things is to take drastic action. They bomb defense factories; they encourage riots and strikes by workers; they phone in bomb threats to airports, government offices, and schools.

_____ A person sells secret but insignificant information to a foreign power.

_____ A person sells secret information which could be severely damaging to her country's safety.

_____ A young man works in a high security defense plant, a job which his father got him. He is approached by spies who ask him to sell them sensitive information. The young man takes pride in selling the best, most top secret information because it pleases the spies. He doesn't really care about how these transactions affect his country.

Now, look at the list of considerations listed below. Which ones were most important in your decisions about the situations described above? Rank these considerations from 1 (most important to you) to 13 (least important to you).

_____ the safety of the nation
_____ the safety of individuals
_____ the personal gain (money or freedom, for example) of the person committing the act
_____ the honesty or dishonesty of the act
_____ whether the person committing the act is native or foreign
_____ the openness or secretiveness of the act
_____ the size of the act or its degree of importance (for example, whether a person gave a little, unimportant information to the enemy or gave a lot of very important information)

165

_____ the degree to which the person seemed to understand the consequences of their actions

_____ your own desire to get revenge on traitors

_____ your own belief in the importance of giving deterrent examples to future would-be traitors

_____ your own belief that the death penalty can never be right

_____ other:

What does this activity tell you about your own values regarding treason and the death penalty?

Compare and discuss your answers with those of other people who have done this activity.

Periodical Bibliography

The following list of periodical articles deals with the subject matter of this chapter.

The Congressional Digest	"The Question of Capital Punishment," August/September 1927.
Edward C. Domaingue II	"A Second Treason," *The Union Leader*, October 31, 1985.
S. Andhil Fineberg	"Plain Facts About the Rosenberg Case," *Reader's Digest*, September 1953.
Morton H. Halperin	"How to Stop the Sale Of Secrets: Don't Go for Easy 'Solutions,'" *The New York Times*, July 22, 1985.
Bobby R. Inman	"The Walker Case: A Direct Hit?" *The Washington Post National Weekly Edition*, June 24, 1985.
Freda Kirchway	"Mercy for the Rosenbergs," *The Nation*, January 10, 1953.
The Literary Digest	"Reaffirming the Guilt of Sacco and Vanzetti," Vol. XCIV, No. 8, August 20, 1927.
W. Luther	"Damage Report on a Spy Ring," *Macleans*, August 5, 1985.
E. Magnuson	"A Spy Ring Goes to Court," *Time*, August 19, 1985.
The Nation	"Justice Underfoot," August 17, 1927.
The Nation	"A Decent Respect to the Opinions of Mankind," August 24, 1927.
National Review	"An Absolute Moral Void," June 28, 1985.
The New Republic	"Radicalism and the Sacco-Vanzetti Case," October 12, 1927.
The New Republic	"The Lesson of It for Liberals," September 28, 1927.
Jacques Nonod	In a "Letter to the Editor," *Bulletin of the Atomic Scientists*, December 1953.
Time	National Affairs Section Under "Espionage," June 29, 1953.
The Washington Times	"A Deal for John Walker," October 30, 1985.

Bibliography of Books

Jack Henry Abbott — *In the Belly of the Beast.* New York: Random House, Inc., 1981.

Johanness Andenaes — *Punishment and Deterrence.* Ann Arbor, MI: University of Michigan Press, 1974.

Hugo Adam Bedau — *The Case Against the Death Penalty.* 1977. Pamphlet available from American Civil Liberties Union, 22 E. Fortieth St., New York, NY 10016.

Hugo Adam Bedau — *The Courts, the Constitution, and Capital Punishment.* Lexington, MA: D.C. Heath and Company, 1977.

Hugo Adam Bedau, ed. — *The Death Penalty in America.* New York: Oxford University Press, 1982.

Larry C. Berkson — *The Concept of Cruel and Unusual Punishment.* Lexington, MA: D.C. Heath and Company, 1975.

Walter Berns — *For Capital Punishment: Crime and the Morality of the Death Penalty.* New York: Basic Books, Inc., 1979.

Charles L. Black — *Capital Punishment: The Inevitability of Caprice and Mistake.* New York: W.W. Norton & Company, Inc., 1974.

Eugene B. Block — *When Men Play God.* San Francisco, CA: Cragmont Publications, 1983.

William J. Bowers — *Legal Homicide: Death as Punishment in America, 1864-1982.* Boston: Northeastern University Press, 1974.

Michael V. DiSalle — *The Power of Life or Death.* New York: Random House, 1965.

Thomas Draper, ed. — *Capital Punishment.* New York: H.H. Wilson Company, 1985.

Michael E. Endres — *The Morality of Capital Punishment: Equal Justice Under the Law.* Mystic, CT: Twenty-Third Publications, 1985.

Lucy Freeman and Wilfred C. Hulse — *Children Who Kill.* New York: Berkley Publishing Company, 1962.

Theodore Heline — *Capital Punishment: Historical Trends Toward Its Abolishment.* Los Angeles, CA: New Age Press, Inc., 1965.

H. Montgomery Hyde	*The Atom Bomb Spies.* New York: Atheneum Press, 1980.
Robert Johnson	*Condemned to Die: Life Under Sentence of Death.* New York: Elsevier North Holland, Inc., 1981.
John Laurence	*A History of Capital Punishment.* New York: The Citadel Press, 1960.
Philip English Mackey	*Voices Against Death.* New York: Burt Franklin & Co., 1976.
Roy Meador	*Capital Revenge: 54 Votes Against Life.* Philadelphia: Dorrance & Company, 1975.
Basil Montague, ed.	*The Opinions of Different Authors upon the Punishment Death.* Vols. 1-3, Buffalo, NY: William S. Hein & Company, 1984.
Ronald Radosh and Joyce Milton	*The Rosenberg File: A Search for the Truth.* New York: Vintage Books, 1984.
Ethel (Greenglass) Rosenberg	*Death House Letters of Ethel and Julius Rosenberg.* New York: Jero Publishing Company, 1953.
Thorsten Sallin	*The Penalty of Death.* Beverly Hills, CA: Sage Publications, 1980.
Malcolm P. Sharp	*Was Justice Done? The Rosenberg-Sobell Case.* New York: Monthly Review Press, 1956.
Mark A. Siegel, and Nancy R. Jacobs, eds.	*Capital Punishment, Cruel and Unusual?* Plano, TX: Instructional Aides, Inc.
Ernest van den Haag and John P. Conrad	*The Death Penalty.* New York: Plenum Press, 1983.
John Wexley	*The Judgement of Julius and Ethel Rosenberg.* New York: Cameron & Kahn, 1955.

Index

173